EYEWITNESS
US PRESIDENTS

Fan commemorating Lincoln

Theodore Roosevelt banner

Carter campaign memorabilia

Anti-Nixon buttons

McKinley campaign umbrella

Penguin Random House

REVISED EDITION

DK DELHI
Senior Art Editor Vikas Chauhan
Editor Aashirwad Jain
Assistant Art Editor Prateek Maurya
Team Lead, Picture Research Sumedha Chopra
Deputy Manager, Picture Research Virien Chopra
Deputy Managing Editor Sreshtha Bhattacharya
Managing Editor Kingshuk Ghoshal
Managing Art Editor Govind Mittal
Production Editor Pawan Kumar
Hi-Res Coordinator Jagtar Singh
Jackets Designer Rashika Kachroo
Creative Head Malavika Talukder

DK LONDON
Project Editor Vicky Richards
Art Editor Chrissy Checketts
Managing Editor Francesca Baines
Managing Art Editor Philip Letsu
Production Controller Jack Matts
Publisher Andrew Macintyre
Art Director Mabel Chan

Consultant Philip Baselice
Authenticity Reader Bianca Hezekiah

FIRST EDITION

Created By Leapfrog Press Ltd.
Senior Editor and Co-Author Bridget Hopkinson
Editor Jacky Jackson
Art Editors Catherine Goldsmith and Adrienne Hutchinson
Art Director Miranda Kennedy

DK Publishing
Publisher Neal Porter **Executive Editor** Iris Rosoff **Art Director** Dirk Kaufman

This edition published in 2025
First published in Great Britain in 2000 by
Dorling Kindersley Limited,
20 Vauxhall Bridge Road,
London SW1V 2SA

The authorised representative in the EEA is
Dorling Kindersley Verlag GmbH. Arnulfstr. 124,
80636 Munich, Germany

Copyright © 2000, 2003, 2009, 2013, 2017, 2021, 2025 Dorling Kindersley Limited
Photographs copyright © 2000, 2003, 2009, 2013, 2017, 2021, 2025 Smithsonian
Institution, except for various photographs – see credits
Compilation copyright © 2000, 2003, 2009, 2013, 2017, 2021, 2025
Dorling Kindersley Limited
A Penguin Random House Company
10 9 8 7 6 5 4 3 2 1
001–345768–Apr/2025

All rights reserved.
No part of this publication may be reproduced, stored in or introduced
into a retrieval system, or transmitted, in any form, or by any means
(electronic, mechanical, photocopying, recording, or otherwise),
without the prior written permission of the copyright owner.

No part of this publication may be used or reproduced
in any manner for the purpose of training artificial intelligence
technologies or systems. In accordance with Article 4(3) of
the DSM Directive 2019/790, DK expressly reserves
this work from the text and data mining exception.

A CIP catalogue record for this book is available from the British Library.
ISBN 978-0-2417-2584-9

Printed and bound in Malaysia

www.dk.com

This book was made with Forest Stewardship Council™ certified paper – one small step in DK's commitment to a sustainable future.
Learn more at www.dk.com/uk/information/sustainability

Carter bumper stickers

Eyeglasses belonging to James K. Polk

Life magazine cover from the Coolidge era

Lewis and Clark compass from Jefferson's presidency

Teddy bear named after Teddy Roosevelt

Contents

George Washington's field kit from the American Revolution

4
George Washington

8
John Adams

10
Thomas Jefferson

14
James Madison, James Monroe, John Quincy Adams

16
Andrew Jackson

18
Martin Van Buren, William Henry Harrison, John Tyler

20
James K. Polk, Zachary Taylor

22
Millard Fillmore, Franklin Pierce, James Buchanan

24
Abraham Lincoln

28
Andrew Johnson, Ulysses S. Grant

30
Rutherford B. Hayes, James A. Garfield, Chester A. Arthur

32
Grover Cleveland, Benjamin Harrison, William McKinley

34
Theodore Roosevelt

36
William H. Taft, Woodrow Wilson

38
Warren G. Harding, Calvin Coolidge, Herbert Hoover

40
Franklin D. Roosevelt

44
Harry S. Truman

46
Dwight D. Eisenhower

48
John F. Kennedy

50
Lyndon B. Johnson

52
Richard M. Nixon

54
Gerald R. Ford, Jimmy Carter

56
Ronald Reagan

58
George H. W. Bush

60
Bill Clinton

62
George W. Bush

64
Barack Obama

66
Donald Trump

68
Joe Biden

70
Presidential speeches

72
Index

George Washington

In 1789, George Washington became the first president of the United States of America. The American colonies had won independence from Great Britain in the American Revolution. Washington, a war hero, was described by Thomas Jefferson as "a wise, a good, and a great man". His example has defined the presidency ever since.

This is the military mess kit that George Washington carried with him in the American Revolution.

Revolutionary leadership

As a young man, Washington became commander of the colonial army in Virginia and fought in the French and Indian War. When the American Revolution began in 1775, he was chosen to lead American forces. Although not a great strategist, he had determination and succeeded in holding his badly equipped army together and securing victory in 1781.

During the war, Washington would have spent hours in this camp tent planning his next move against the British.

Patriot medal celebrating an early victory over the British at Boston in March 1776

Crossing the Delaware River

Defeated at Long Island in August 1776, the Patriot cause seemed lost, until Washington struck back. On 25 December, he led his army across the river at night. Surprising the British soldiers, he won a victory at Trenton, New Jersey.

General Washington leads his troops across the Delaware River on Christmas Day, 1776.

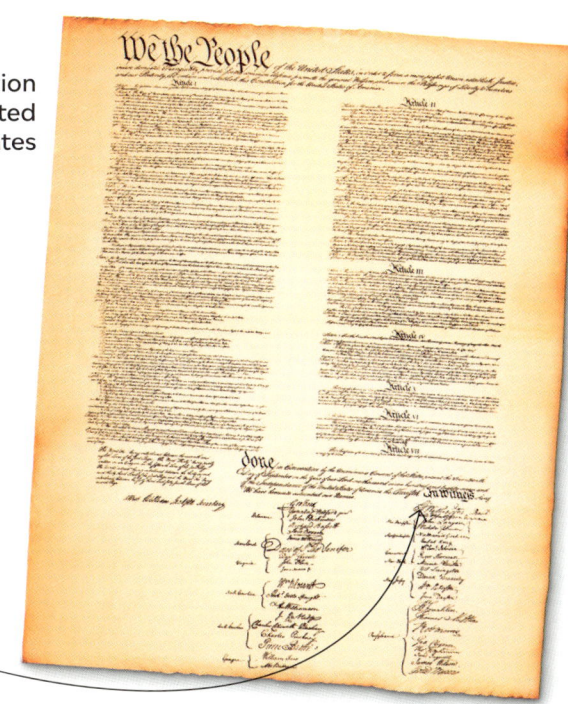

The Constitution of the United States

George Washington's signature

Drafting the Constitution

In 1787, Washington presided over the Constitutional Convention in Philadelphia and helped draft a new system of democratic government. It had three branches: the Senate and the House of Representatives would make the laws in the legislative branch, the Supreme Court would dispense justice in the judicial branch, and the president would enforce the laws in the executive branch.

Buttons celebrating Washington's inauguration

The new president

George Washington's powers as president were clearly set out under the new Constitution. He had the power to appoint high-ranking government officials, command the armed forces, and make treaties with other countries. The Constitution stated that each president should serve a four-year term of office and then stand for re-election. Washington did this, and after two terms, he decided that he had served long enough.

In a tradition he started, George Washington swears an oath on the Bible, becoming the first US president.

George Washington was unanimously **chosen twice** as the US president.

Washington at home

George Washington grew up on a farm in Virginia. Aged 20, he inherited the Mount Vernon estate and became one of the largest landowners in northern Virginia. He considered farming "the most noble employment of man". When at home, he spent his days running the plantation and pursuing sports such as hunting and fishing. In his later years, he and his wife, Martha, spent much of their of time entertaining the many guests who visited Mount Vernon.

Mount Vernon
Spanning 3,240 hectares (8,000 acres), Mount Vernon was an extremely large plantation. Washington used forced labour of enslaved people to plant trees, wheat, and vegetables. He also had enslaved people working inside the house.

Washington with his wife, Martha, and two of her grandchildren, c.1796

- George Washington
- Washington liked fine clothes and ordered most of his coats from London.
- William Lee, an enslaved person at Mount Vernon
- Martha Washington had a dignified bearing.
- Eleanor Parke Custis
- John Parke Custis

Martha Washington
In 1759, Washington married a widow, Martha Dandridge Custis, and became father to Martha's two children from her first marriage. Martha grew into her role as first lady, hosting official receptions with great decorum.

Presidential entertaining
Washington believed that as president he should behave with reserve and dignity. He was formal with colleagues. Dinners were formal as well, with guests referring to their hosts as President and Lady Washington.

The Whiskey Rebellion
In 1794, Washington's authority was tested when a rebellion broke out in Pennsylvania over a new federal whiskey tax. The governor of Pennsylvania refused to enforce the tax, so Washington led an army to ensure that the law was obeyed.

A federal officer tarred and feathered by angry farmers

US officers at the Battle of Fallen Timbers, 1794

Territory wars

White settlers moving onto territory stolen from Indigenous Peoples caused many conflicts. When US troops were ambushed by Indigenous Peoples of the Northwest Confederation, Washington sent reinforcements, resulting in a US victory at the Battle of Fallen Timbers. The Confederation lost Ohio in the Treaty of Fort Greenville in 1795.

Seneca leader Sagoyewatha was one of the leaders of the Six Nations.

Early treaty

In 1794, US negotiators met leaders of the Haudenosaunee Confederacy (or Six Nations), who agreed to grant land concessions to the US in exchange for promises of friendship, peace, and the US respecting their remaining lands.

Childhood myth

In *Life of Washington* (1806), the author Mason Locke Weems made up an event to show the leader's honesty. A young Washington reputedly cut down his father's cherry tree. When asked, he said: "I cannot tell a lie. I did it".

George Washington on a banknote, 1800

The legend of Washington

George Washington became a legend in his lifetime. He had endured the trials of war and had shown great courage and purpose in helping to forge a nation. Known as the "Father of His Country", Washington's image appeared on everything, from porcelain to money.

Handkerchief with a map of Washington, D.C.

The nation's capital

In 1791, George Washington helped select a site on the Potomac River to be the nation's capital. In his honour, the city was named Washington.

GEORGE WASHINGTON

1ST PRESIDENT
1789–1797

BORN
22 February 1732
Westmoreland County, Virginia

INAUGURATED AS PRESIDENT
First term: 30 April 1789
Second term: 4 March 1793

AGE AT INAUGURATION
57

PARTY
Independent

FIRST LADY
Martha Dandridge Custis

CHILDREN ADOPTED BY MARRIAGE
John Parke Custis
Martha Parke Custis

DIED
14 December 1799
Mount Vernon, Virginia

KEY EVENTS OF PRESIDENCY

1789 Washington appoints Thomas Jefferson as secretary of state and Alexander Hamilton as secretary of the treasury; John Adams is vice president.

1791 A national bank is established; the site for the nation's new capital, Washington, D.C., is selected; the first 10 amendments of the Constitution are ratified.

1792 Congress establishes a national mint.

1793 Washington issues the Proclamation of Neutrality to avoid conflict with Britain and France, who are at war.

1794 Washington signs the Jay Treaty with Great Britain, allowing US ships to be inspected at sea in return for the removal of British troops from the Northwest Territory.

John Adams

John Adams was not a popular hero like George Washington. He could be pompous and had many political enemies. Yet, he was a Founding Father of the country and helped draft the Declaration of Independence. He felt overlooked as vice president, claiming the role was "the most insignificant office that ever the invention of man contrived". But his loyalty was rewarded. In 1797, Adams became president. Foreign affairs dominated his term of office.

John Adams had a proud personality.

His Rotundity
John Adams was born in Braintree, Massachusetts, and studied law at Harvard University. By his own admission, he was "puffy, vain, conceited". Adams' detractors referred to him as "His Rotundity".

Father of the Navy
When Adams became president, Britain and France were at war. After France attacked US ships to stop them from trading with Britain, Adams established a naval branch of the military. For two years, French and US frigates fought at sea. In 1800, Adams negotiated an end to hostilities.

Cookbook used in the Adams family, c. 1780

Abigail Adams
While Adams was away, his wife Abigail ran their farm and wrote constantly to her husband advising him on political matters. Their marriage was a happy one, lasting more than 50 years.

Vest belonging to John Adams

Alexander Hamilton

Party politics
In Adams' time, two political parties were formed. The Federalists, led by Alexander Hamilton (above), believed in a strong central government. The Democratic-Republicans, led by Thomas Jefferson, favoured the rights of states to decide matters concerning themselves. Adams was often caught in the middle.

The frigate USS Constitution *was first launched in 1797. After restoration, she sailed again in 1997.*

JOHN ADAMS

2ND PRESIDENT
1797–1801

BORN
30 October 1735
Braintree (now Quincy), Massachusetts

INAUGURATED AS PRESIDENT
4 March 1797

AGE AT INAUGURATION
61

PARTY
Federalist

FIRST LADY
Abigail Smith

CHILDREN
Abigail Amelia
John Quincy
Susanna
Charles
Thomas Boylston

DIED
4 July 1826
Quincy, Massachusetts

Fit for a president
In 1800, Adams transferred the federal government to Washington, D.C., and moved into the unfinished presidential residence.

Thomas Jefferson

Banner commemorating Jefferson's election, 1800

Thomas Jefferson believed in a national government that had limited powers over the states and the people. Yet, as president, he made bold decisions for the country. In 1803, he bought the rights to the vast territory of Louisiana from France for 15 million dollars. This doubled the size of the US and made westward expansion possible. He stepped down after eight years in office.

Jefferson the patriot

At the start of the American Revolution, Jefferson served in the Continental Congress, which acted on behalf of the colonies. In 1784, he joined John Adams and Benjamin Franklin in Europe to negotiate treaties with European powers. Jefferson returned in 1789 to take up his role as secretary of state. In 1801, he became president.

Jefferson (right) writing the Declaration of Independence with John Adams (centre) and Benjamin Franklin (left)

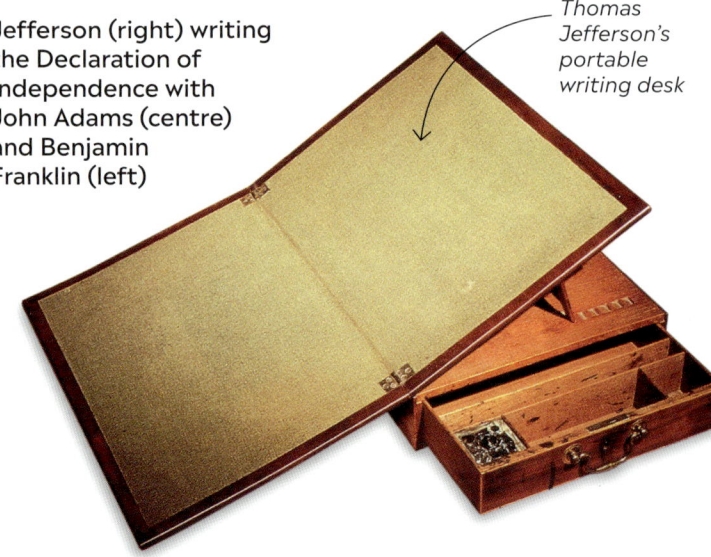
Thomas Jefferson's portable writing desk

The Declaration of Independence

At the Continental Congress in 1776, Jefferson was asked to write the Declaration of Independence. In this historic document, he stated that all people had certain basic rights to life and liberty. The Declaration was addressed to the British king, George III, whom the Americans accused of stepping on their rights. They argued that the American colonies should be "free and independent states".

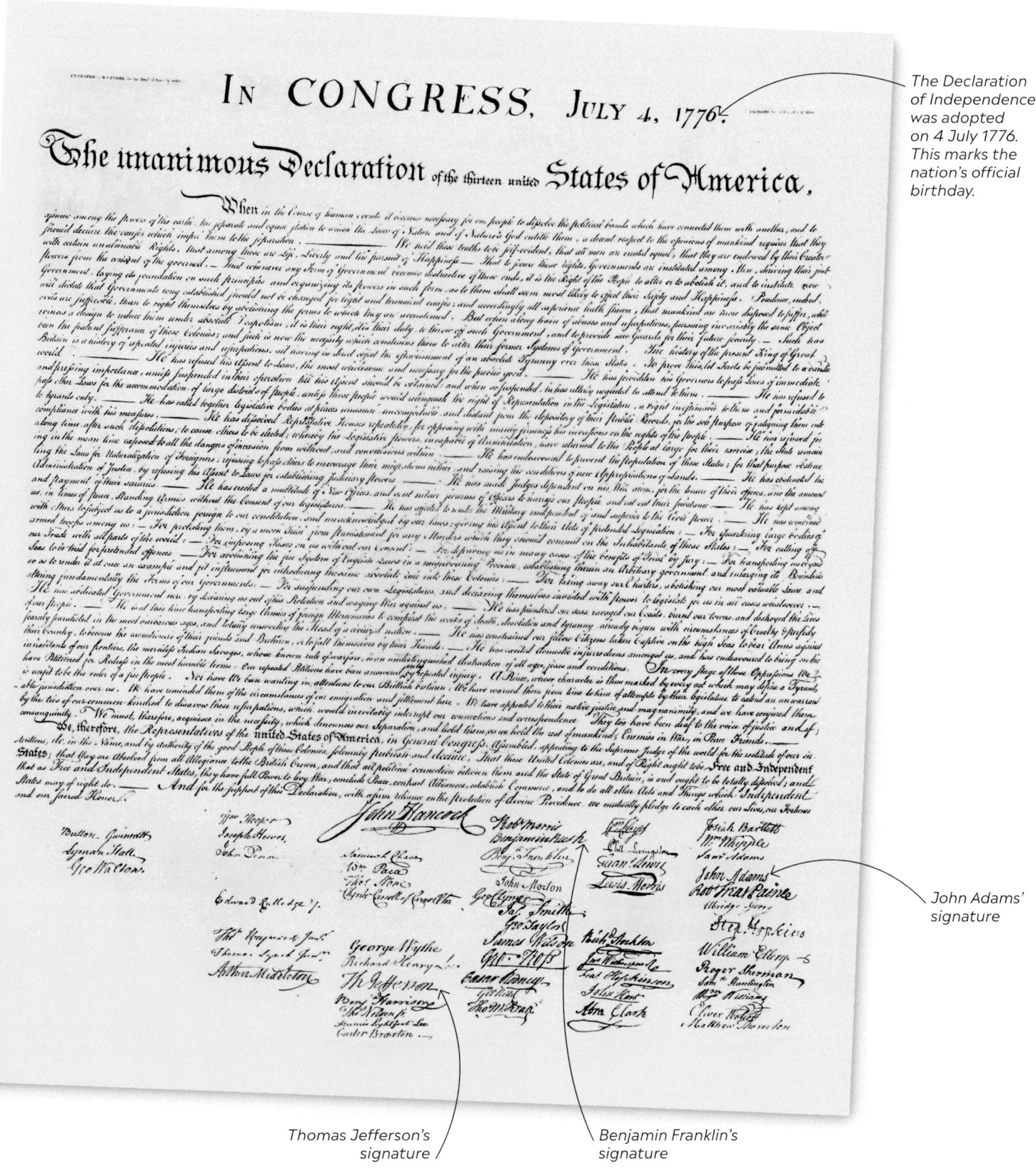

The Declaration of Independence was adopted on 4 July 1776. This marks the nation's official birthday.

John Adams' signature

Thomas Jefferson's signature

Benjamin Franklin's signature

Continued from previous page

Great scholar

Jefferson was one of the most learned men in US history. He knew six languages; studied music, law, science, and philosophy; and was a self-taught architect. He amassed three libraries in his lifetime, the second of which was sold to the US government to start the Library of Congress.

Monticello

Inspired by the 16th-century Italian architect Andrea Palladio, Jefferson designed his home on a hill above Charlottesville, Virginia. He named it Monticello, Italian for "little mountain". He designed many features for the house, such as a dumbwaiter, swivel chairs, and alcove beds.

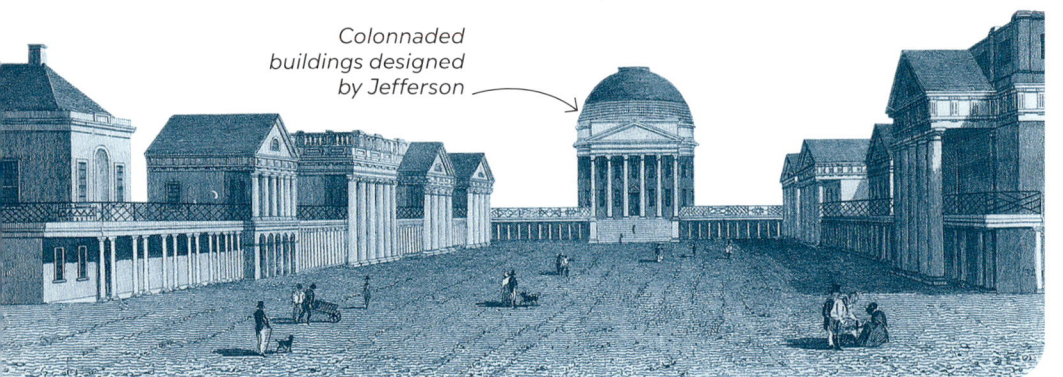

Colonnaded buildings designed by Jefferson

The University of Virginia

Jefferson believed strongly in education. One of his proudest achievements was founding the University of Virginia. He planned the curriculum and even designed the buildings.

Sacagawea became a heroine in national folklore.

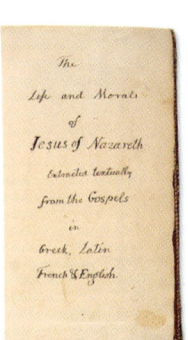

The Jefferson Bible

Jefferson and religion

In an 1802 letter to the Danbury Baptist Church, Jefferson first defined the concept that would become a core American value: the separation of church and state. He believed there should be a wall between people's religious beliefs and the laws US citizens must follow.

Jefferson's gravestone

All men are created equal

Jefferson died on 4 July 1826, leaving a mixed legacy. Although he spent his life fighting for freedom and equality, he did not extend the same freedom to the more than 600 enslaved people on whose forced labour he relied.

The Lewis and Clark Expedition

An avid amateur naturalist, Jefferson was eager to find out about the American West. In 1804, he sent an expedition, led by Meriwether Lewis and William Clark, to explore the newly acquired Louisiana Territory. Lewis and Clark were aided by a Shoshone diplomat named Sacagawea, who helped them communicate with the different Indigenous Peoples they met. Over two years, the team travelled as far as the Pacific Ocean, keeping detailed accounts of the plants and animals they saw.

One of the compasses carried by the Lewis and Clark Expedition

Meriwether Lewis was appointed governor of the Louisiana Territory upon his return in 1806.

William Clark became Superintendent of Indian Affairs in the Louisiana Territory and, later, governor of the Missouri Territory.

THOMAS JEFFERSON

3RD PRESIDENT
1801–1809

BORN
13 April 1743
Albemarle County, Virginia

INAUGURATED AS PRESIDENT
First term: 4 March 1801
Second term: 4 March 1805

AGE AT INAUGURATION
57

PARTY
Democratic-Republican

WIFE
Martha Wayles Skelton
(died 1782)

CHILDREN
Martha
Mary
Lucy Elizabeth

DIED
4 July 1826
Charlottesville, Virginia

KEY EVENTS OF PRESIDENCY

1803 In the *Marbury v. Madison* case, the Supreme Court declares an act of Congress to be unconstitutional for the first time; Jefferson makes the Louisiana Purchase.

1804 Jefferson is re-elected as president; Jefferson's rival, Aaron Burr, kills Secretary of the Treasury Alexander Hamilton in a duel.

1806 Aaron Burr tries to incite a rebellion in Louisiana.

1807 Burr is tried for treason, but is acquitted; the US frigate *Chesapeake* is fired upon and boarded by a British warship; Jefferson bans the export of US goods to Europe in retaliation for the *Chesapeake* incident.

1808 Jefferson prohibits importing enslaved people from Africa.

James Madison

James Madison was a great political thinker. In 1787, he was a leader in framing the Constitution and was nicknamed the "Father of the Constitution". After serving as Secretary of State for eight years, Madison became president in 1809. During his administration, the US became involved in the War of 1812 with Britain. The war went badly for the US and people referred to it bitterly as "Mr Madison's War". His reputation was rescued, in part, when US troops won the Battle of New Orleans in 1815.

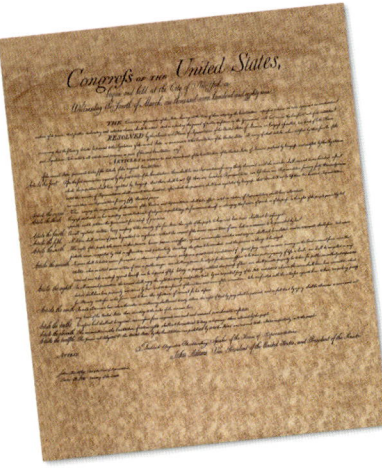

The Bill of Rights
In the 1780s, Madison led the fight to have safeguards built into the Constitution. The first 10 amendments, known as the Bill of Rights (1791), allowed freedom of speech, religion, and assembly, and the right to trial by jury.

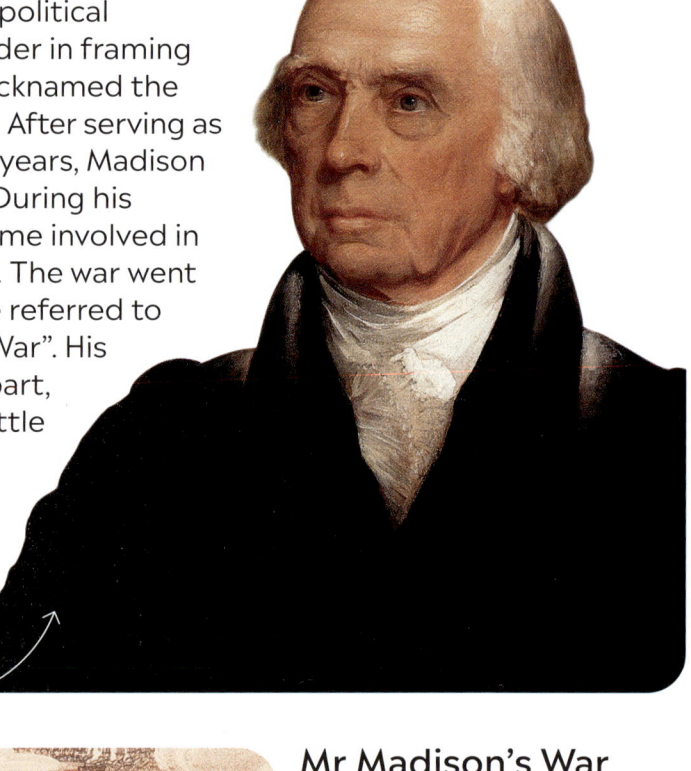

In stature, James Madison was the nation's smallest president. Barely 1.6 m (5 ft 4 in) tall, he weighed only about 45.3 kg (100 lb).

Mr Madison's War
In June 1812, a group of politicians known as the War Hawks pushed for war on Great Britain. There were reasons for the war – British harassment of US ships and the kidnapping of American sailors – but Madison was reluctant. The country was ill-prepared to fight, and the war went badly for the US.

The British Army lost three generals at the Battle of New Orleans in 1815.

Washington in flames
The year 1814 was bleak for President Madison. In August, British forces burned the capital, Washington, D.C. A peace treaty was signed later that year, but neither the US nor Great Britain could be said to have won the war.

A courageous first lady
Dolley Madison was a popular first lady. When the British invaded Washington, D.C., Dolley packed up the national seal, her husband's papers, and a portrait of George Washington, and sent them on ahead before leaving. Shortly after, British troops set fire to the White House.

James Monroe

James Monroe was the last of the Revolutionary Patriots to become president. His presidency was known as the "Era of Good Feelings", because the nation was at peace. Yet, not everything was ideal. There was a depression in 1819, and the Missouri Compromise of 1820 ignited debates about whether the practice of enslavement would be allowed in the new states and territories. Monroe is best remembered, though, for his foreign policy doctrine.

Serious by nature, Monroe proved to be a popular president.

The Monroe Doctrine
The Monroe Doctrine (1823) stated that the US would not tolerate Europe trying to establish further colonies or intervene in the Americas. In return, the US would not interfere in Europe.

John Quincy Adams

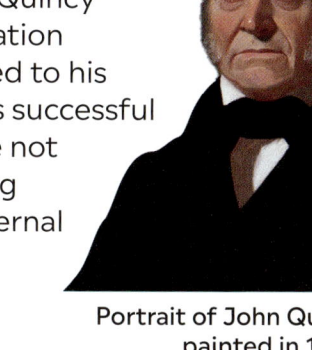

John Quincy Adams was the son of former president John Adams. Like his father, John Quincy Adams had a reserved personality. His education and talent for learning languages contributed to his success as a diplomat. Yet, Adams was not as successful as president. He found that the people were not interested in his advanced ideas for spending their taxes on scientific explorations and internal improvements, such as roads and canals. Adams was not re-elected.

Portrait of John Quincy Adams painted in 1844

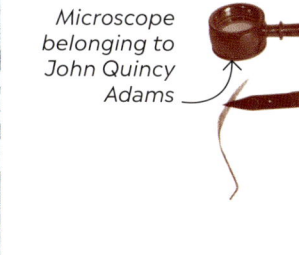

Microscope belonging to John Quincy Adams

The last days
After losing re-election in 1828, John Quincy Adams began a distinguished career in the House of Representatives, where he was a vigorous opponent of slavery. In 1848, at age 80, Adams suffered a stroke while in the House and died two days later.

JAMES MADISON
4TH PRESIDENT
1809–1817

BORN
16 March 1751
Port Conway, Virginia

DIED
28 June 1836
Montpelier, Virginia

JAMES MONROE
5TH PRESIDENT
1817–1825

BORN
28 April 1758, Westmoreland County, Virginia

DIED
4 July 1831
New York, New York

JOHN QUINCY ADAMS
6TH PRESIDENT
1825–1829

BORN
11 July 1767
Quincy, Massachusetts

DIED
23 February 1848
Washington, D.C.

Andrew Jackson

Andrew Jackson was the first president born in a log cabin, and he brought a frontier spirit to the White House. He represented ordinary citizens and vetoed legislation that favoured the wealthy, a policy known as "Jacksonian democracy". He also pushed for the elimination of the property ownership requirement to vote. A popular president, Jackson was easily re-elected.

Snuff box showing Jackson as a war hero

Comb bearing Jackson's image

Inauguration Day antics
On Inauguration Day, rowdy supporters crowded into the White House to celebrate. Jackson was forced to flee.

A battlefield hero as president
Despite being born into poverty and receiving little education, Jackson became a very wealthy man. After working as a slave trader, he became a successful lawyer and was appointed a judge in Tennessee. He resigned in 1804 to start a cotton plantation, the Hermitage. By 1820, he had 100 enslaved people working the fields. He was also a military leader, and earned the nickname "Hero of New Orleans" for defeating the British during the War of 1812.

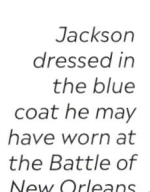

ANDREW JACKSON

7TH PRESIDENT
1829–1837

BORN
15 March 1767
The Waxhaws, South Carolina

INAUGURATED AS PRESIDENT
First term: 4 March 1829
Second term: 4 March 1833

AGE AT INAUGURATION
61

PARTY
Democratic

WIFE
Rachel Donelson Robards
(died 1828)

ADOPTED
Andrew Jackson, Jr

DIED
8 June 1845
Nashville, Tennessee

Jackson dressed in the blue coat he may have worn at the Battle of New Orleans

All 183 of the Texas rebels were killed.

King Andrew

Many politicians thought Jackson abused his position in the name of the people. In their opinion, he vetoed legislation as he saw fit, rather than giving in to the will of Congress. His enemies named him "King Andrew", implying that he behaved more like a king than as an elected president.

This cartoon portrays Jackson as a king with a sceptre in one hand and a document declaring his power of veto in the other.

The Alamo

When Jackson became president, the land that makes up Texas belonged to Mexico. When Mexico outlawed slavery in Texas, a group of furious white enslavers captured San Antonio, leading to the siege of the Alamo. During the siege, all the rebels were killed. Six weeks later, the Texans defeated the Mexicans and won independence. They were also granted the legal right to own enslaved people again.

Driven out

In 1830, Jackson signed the Indian Removal Act, forcibly removing Indigenous Peoples from their homelands to the uninhabited frontier. This forced migration, known as the Trail of Tears, resulted in the deaths of thousands of Indigenous people due to disease and starvation.

Duelling pistols c. 1800

Too quick to shoot

Jackson had a very temperamental nature and was prone to extreme violence. He once shot and killed a man in a duel over an unkind remark about his wife, Rachel.

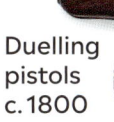

Gold epaulets

Chief John Ross, the leader of the Cherokee Nation, tried unsuccessfully to oppose Jackson's plan of forcing his people to move.

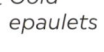

The Hermitage

Jackson lived with his wife at the Hermitage, a plantation home near Nashville that relied on the forced labour of enslaved people.

This humorous 1834 biography of Jackson satirizes the president.

Martin Van Buren

Martin Van Buren was known for his political cunning. Having served as Andrew Jackson's trusted vice president, Jackson chose him to be the next president. Unfortunately, an economic depression followed Van Buren to the White House. When he was unable to bring back prosperity, he was voted out of office.

A photograph, or daguerreotype, of Van Buren in later years

Champagne-drinking president

Van Buren was often criticized for his expensive tastes. During the election campaign of 1840, he was portrayed as a dandy who dressed himself in finery while the country was in the midst of an economic depression.

Van Buren frowns when he tastes common cider...

...and smiles when he sips champagne!

Campaign item from the 1840 election

Trail of Tears

Van Buren continued Andrew Jackson's policy of forcibly removing Indigenous Peoples. Nearly 59,000 Cherokee, Creek, Seminole, Chickasaw, and Choctaw people were driven from their homelands. They were forced to march without rest, and thousands died along the way in a journey that became known as the Trail of Tears.

In 1838-1839, 15,000 Cherokee were forcibly escorted by federal troops from their homelands to reservations in what is now Oklahoma.

The Cherokee were forced to travel in the bitter cold of autumn and winter with inadequate food supplies.

William Henry Harrison

William Henry Harrison was born on a plantation in Virginia. In 1811, Harrison defeated Chief Tecumseh and the Shawnee people at the Battle of Tippecanoe, leading him to be considered a military hero. Harrison is, however, largely remembered today for serving the shortest term of any president.

MARTIN VAN BUREN
8TH PRESIDENT
1837–1841

BORN
5 December 1782
Kinderhook, New York

DIED
24 July 1862
Kinderhook, New York

WILLIAM HENRY HARRISON
9TH PRESIDENT
1841

BORN
9 February 1773
Berkeley, Virginia

DIED
4 April 1841
Washington, D.C.

JOHN TYLER
10TH PRESIDENT
1841–1845

BORN
29 March 1790
Charles City County, Virginia

DIED
18 January 1862
Richmond, Virginia

Log cabin campaign
In the election of 1840, Harrison's supporters led people to believe their candidate had grown up poor in a log cabin, instead of in a mansion.

Harrison was the first president to die in office.

Illness
Harrison developed pneumonia after delivering the longest inaugural address ever on a freezing March day. He died, at age 68, exactly one month after his inauguration.

John Tyler

Upon Harrison's death, John Tyler became the first vice president to become president. He belonged to the Whig Party, yet did not support many of the Whigs' policies. Worse still, Tyler supported slavery, which many Whigs denounced. He became an outcast in his own party and was removed from it in 1842. He remained party-less while still in office.

Tyler's critics challenged his right to presidency and called him "His Accidency".

A new precedent
After Harrison's death, Tyler quickly assumed the role of president, exercising all the powers and privileges of the office. He set a precedent for future vice presidents.

The new Mrs Tyler
John Tyler was the first president to be married while in office. In 1844, he married the vivacious Julia Gardiner, who was 30 years his junior.

James K Polk

James K Polk believed that the US should fulfill its "destiny" of expanding to the Pacific Ocean. In 1846, a border dispute in Texas triggered a war with Mexico. At the Treaty of Guadalupe Hidalgo (1848), the victorious Americans acquired what is today California, New Mexico, Arizona, Nevada, and Utah. In the Pacific Northwest, Polk settled a long dispute with Great Britain over the Oregon Territory. When he left office, the country spanned two oceans.

JAMES K POLK

11TH PRESIDENT
1845–1849

BORN
2 November 1795
Mecklenburg County,
North Carolina

INAUGURATED AS PRESIDENT
4 March 1845

AGE AT INAUGURATION
49

PARTY
Democratic

FIRST LADY
Sarah Childress

CHILDREN
None

DIED
15 June 1849
Nashville, Tennessee

1,000 Colt revolvers were issued to US soldiers in the Mexican-American War.

The Mexican-American War

President Polk tried to buy the southwestern territories from Mexico. When that failed, he instigated the Mexican-American War. The leadership of future president General Zachary Taylor and the US Army's superior weaponry led to Mexico's defeat in 1848.

General Zachary Taylor's faithful horse, Whitey, was almost as famous as his owner during the war.

General Taylor

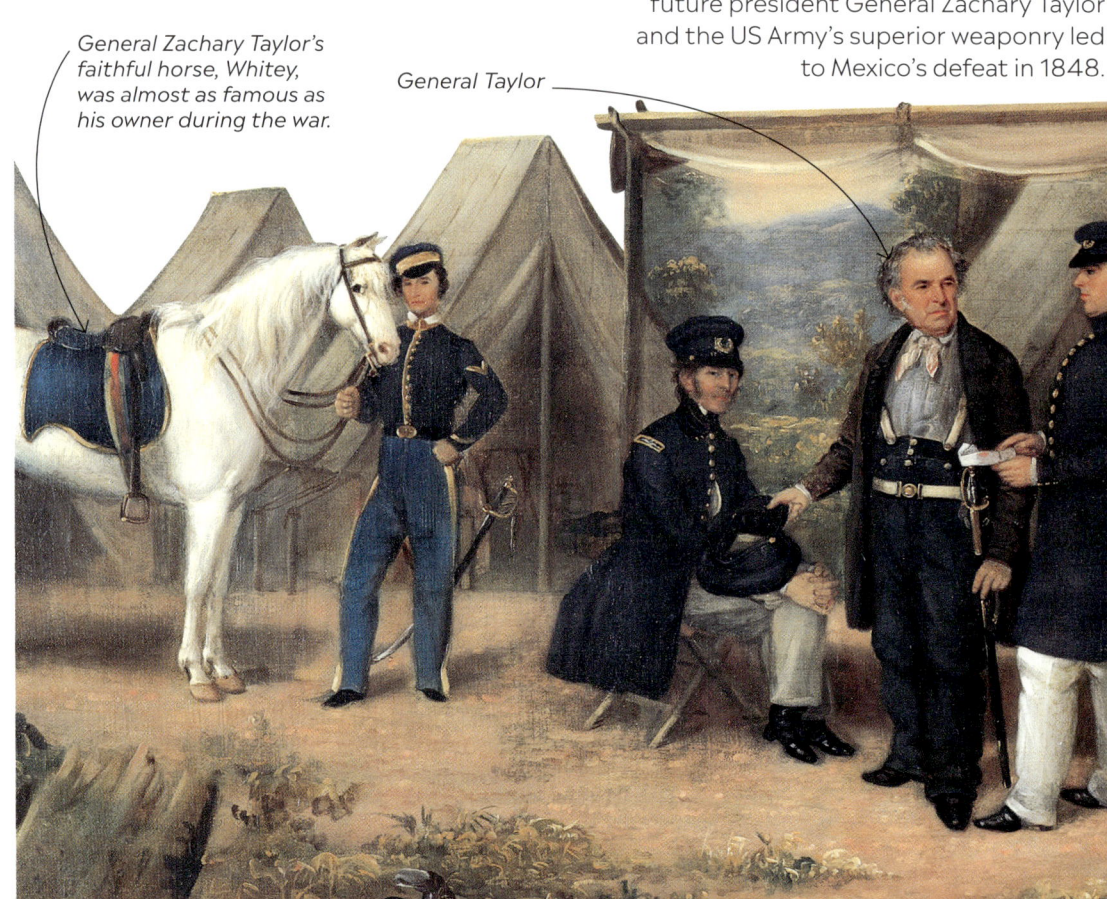

Zachary Taylor

Nicknamed "Old Rough and Ready", Zachary Taylor became president in 1848. Taylor did not want the new southwestern territories to become slave states, despite owning more than 100 enslaved people himself. He threatened to veto the Compromise of 1850, which admitted some territories as slave states and some as free because he thought it favoured the slave states.

Although he looks sharp in this portrait, Taylor was often dressed in rumpled clothes.

Gold miners were called Forty-Niners after the year they arrived in California.

Gold rush
When gold was discovered in California in 1848 and 1849, thousands of people poured into the territory hoping to make their fortunes. Taylor wanted California to enter the US as a free (non-slave) state.

Buena Vista veteran
Taylor was a veteran of the War of 1812, the Black Hawk War in 1832, and the Seminole War in Florida in 1836–1837. He was also considered a hero for his victories in the Mexican-American War, notably at the Battle of Buena Vista, where he defeated the superior forces of General Santa Anna. When he died in 1850, thousands of mourners lined the route of his funeral procession.

Taylor with members of his staff at his military encampment during the Mexican-American War

ZACHARY TAYLOR

12TH PRESIDENT
1849–1850

BORN
24 November 1784
Montebello, Virginia

INAUGURATED AS PRESIDENT
5 March 1849

AGE AT INAUGURATION
64

PARTY
Whig

FIRST LADY
Margaret Mackall Smith

CHILDREN
Ann Mackall
Sarah Knox
Octavia Pannill
Margaret Smith
Mary Elizabeth
Richard

DIED
9 July 1850
Washington, D.C.

Leg irons were used to restrain enslaved people.

Portrait of Fillmore, c. 1840

Millard Fillmore

Millard Fillmore grew up poor on a farm in New York state. He favoured the Compromise of 1850, which temporarily kept the Union together. By signing the Fugitive Slave Act, however, he lost the support of the northerners in his Whig party and was voted out of office in 1852.

Perry's mission to Japan
In 1853, Fillmore sent Commodore Perry to open trade links with the Japanese, who refused to trade with other nations. Intimidated by US naval power, the emperor agreed to open Japan's ports after the Kanagawa Treaty in 1854.

The Fugitive Slave Act
The most controversial part of the Compromise of 1850 was the Fugitive Slave Act. It promised federal support for returning enslaved people who had escaped to enslavers, allowing those who had run away to be hunted down in the North. Abolitionists were outraged.

Uncle Tom's Cabin
Harriet Beecher Stowe was an abolitionist (someone who wanted to end slavery). Her 1852 novel *Uncle Tom's Cabin* brought the issue of enslavement to the forefront of public attention.

MILLARD FILLMORE
13TH PRESIDENT
1850–1853

BORN
7 January 1800
Cayuga County, New York

DIED
8 March 1874
Buffalo, New York

FRANKLIN PIERCE
14TH PRESIDENT
1853–1857

BORN
23 November 1804
Hillsboro, New Hampshire

DIED
8 October 1869
Concord, New Hampshire

JAMES BUCHANAN
15TH PRESIDENT
1857–1861

BORN
23 April 1791
Cove Gap, Pennsylvania

DIED
1 June 1868
Lancaster, Pennsylvania

Franklin Pierce

Franklin Pierce tried to keep peace between the North and the South, yet he made a fateful decision in supporting the Kansas-Nebraska Act (1854). This act allowed settlers to decide whether or not to allow slavery in their territories. It provoked fighting in what became known as "Bleeding Kansas". The country stepped closer to war.

Daguerreotype (image created on a metal plate) of Pierce, c. 1852; his nickname was "Handsome Frank".

Senate attack
During the passage of the Kansas-Nebraska Act, Southern representative Preston Brooks brutally attacked anti-slavery senator Charles Sumner.

Bleeding Kansas
In 1855, thousands of people from Missouri (a pro-slavery state) voted in Kansas against the Free-Soil (anti-slavery) Party. When a pro-slavery government was elected in Kansas, a border war broke out.

"Border Ruffians" from Missouri

James Buchanan

The presidency of James Buchanan was doomed from the start. For 10 years, the slavery debate had troubled the White House. Buchanan argued that slavery was legal, and urged compromise. But the abolitionist movement was growing, and across the US, resentment and tensions were building. When he left office, war had become inevitable.

Buchanan, a courtly mannered bachelor, worked as a public servant for 40 years.

Campaign flag for James Buchanan

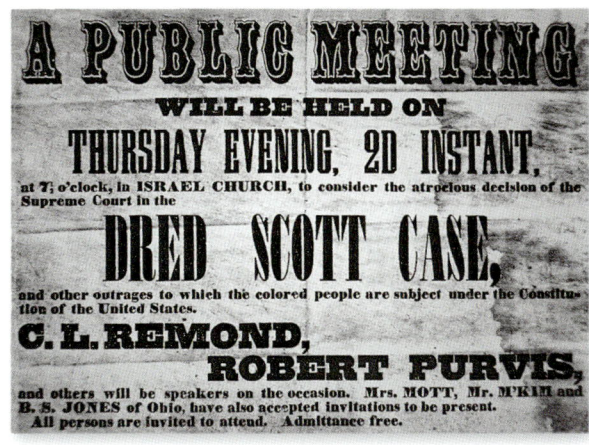

The Dred Scott decision

In 1857, an enslaved man, Dred Scott, sued for his freedom because he had lived in a free state. The Supreme Court ruled that Scott was not a citizen and so could not file a lawsuit. The decision set a precedent that the Constitution did not provide citizenship for free Black people or enslaved people.

John Brown's raid

In 1859, abolitionist John Brown attempted to start a rebellion among enslaved people. His aim was to capture the federal arsenal at Harper's Ferry, Virginia, and mount raids against the owners of enslaved people. Brown was captured and hanged.

Free-Soil Party

In 1858, the pro-slavery constitution in Kansas was voted out. The Free-Soil Party joined the newly formed Republican Party, which promoted the anti-slavery cause in the 1860 election. That year, Republican candidate Abraham Lincoln was elected president. Kansas joined the Union as a free state in 1861.

Free-Soil activists in Kansas armed with a cannon

Frederick Douglass

A formerly enslaved man, Douglass was a prominent Black abolitionist. A brilliant writer and public speaker, he directly opposed the idea – touted by white supremacists and enslavers – that Black people were not intelligent.

Abraham Lincoln

Born in 1809, Abraham Lincoln grew up on the frontier. A former lawyer, he became president in 1860. Though he believed it to be sanctioned by the Constitution, Lincoln deplored slavery. When the Southern states left the Union, Lincoln faced a country on the brink of civil war. It became his mission to reunite the nation. Union victories in the war enabled him to end slavery as well.

Mary Todd Lincoln
Lincoln's wife Mary found her role as first lady difficult. Both the Civil War (she was a Southerner) and the death of her son Willie in 1862 took a toll on her fragile mental health.

A wooden axe carried in campaign parades

Honest Abe
In the campaign of 1860, Lincoln was presented as a good man who had worked his way up through honest labour. He was nicknamed the "Prince of Rails", in reference to an early job as a rail-splitter. Lincoln also worked as a surveyor, a postmaster, and a store clerk, before becoming a lawyer.

Lincoln's clothes often appeared ill-fitting, and he was criticized for his homely appearance.

An unlikely leader
An ambitious young man, Lincoln was a self-trained lawyer and, later, a member of Congress. Although one of the greatest presidents in American history, Lincoln did not cut a dashing figure. At 1.9 m (6 ft 4 in), he often appeared awkward, and spoke with a "frontier" accent.

Lincoln and slavery

The South relied on enslaved labour to produce the crops on which its economy depended. Although Lincoln did not view Black people as equals, he considered slavery unjust. However, he did not want to force the South to abolish slavery. He wanted only to prevent new territories in the West from becoming slave states.

Many enslaved people escaped to the free states in the North via the Underground Railroad, a system of safe houses operated by abolitionists.

A group of Black people who escaped slavery

The Union collapses

In 1861, most Southern states chose to secede, or separate, from the Union. Lincoln did not believe the South had a constitutional right to secede. He had sworn to uphold the laws of the land and was determined to reunite the country, even if it meant war.

South Carolina was the first state to secede, as announced in the Charleston Mercury newspaper.

Jefferson Davis

In February 1861, delegates from the Confederate States met in Montgomery, Alabama, to elect a president. They chose Jefferson Davis of Mississippi. Davis had entered Congress in 1845 and was a commander in the Mexican-American War. Davis was a slave owner and supported the continuation of slavery.

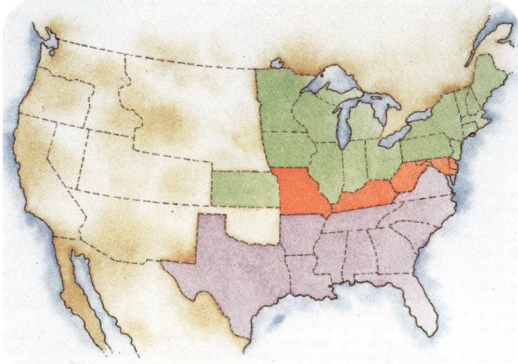

A nation divided

In 1861, seven Southern states seceded to form the Confederate States of America. After war broke out, four more states seceded and joined the CSA (purple). The west part of Virginia seceded from Virginia and remained in the Union (green) joining four slave-owning states that did not secede (red).

ABRAHAM LINCOLN

16TH PRESIDENT
1861–1865

BORN
12 February 1809
Hardin County, Kentucky

INAUGURATED AS PRESIDENT
First term: 4 March 1861
Second term: 4 March 1865

AGE AT INAUGURATION
52

PARTY
Republican

FIRST LADY
Mary Todd

CHILDREN
Robert Todd
Edward Baker
William Wallace
Thomas (Tad)

DIED
15 April 1865
Washington, D.C.

KEY EVENTS OF PRESIDENCY

1861 Eleven Southern states secede from the Union to create the Confederate States of America; Jefferson Davis is elected president of the Confederacy; Civil War erupts; the Union Army is defeated at the first battle of Bull Run.

1862 The Confederates are stopped at Antietam; the Union Army is defeated at Fredericksburg.

1863 Lincoln issues his Emancipation Proclamation, freeing all enslaved people in areas of rebellion; the Confederates are defeated at Gettysburg; Ulysses S. Grant wins at Vicksburg.

1864 Lincoln is re-elected.

1865 General Lee surrenders at Appomattox; Lincoln is assassinated.

Continued from previous page

The Civil War

On 12 April 1861, Confederates fired on Fort Sumter, a Union stronghold in Charleston, South Carolina, forcing the Union soldiers to evacuate. The attack was a near-bloodless beginning to the bloodiest conflict in US history. The vicious fighting was to last four agonizing years. Lincoln was deeply pained by the bloodshed. But he never lost faith, and under his leadership, the Union prevailed.

Union uniform cap, called a kepi

Confederate uniform kepi

Accurate guns with grooved barrels were used in war for the first time, resulting in heavy losses.

This bullet-torn Confederate jacket was found on the battlefield of Seven Pines, Virginia.

Abraham Lincoln and General George B. McClellan at the battlefield of Antietam, Maryland, 3 October 1862

On the battlefield

The Civil War was one of America's most bitter conflicts. Soldiers on both sides fought fiercely. Because of new weapons, losses were heavy. At the Battle of Gettysburg, more than 50,000 men died. Some 600,000 soldiers – two per cent of the population – died in the war.

Engraving portraying Lincoln signing the Emancipation Proclamation

Seeking freedom

Lincoln's Emancipation Proclamation of 1863 declared the enslaved people in the Confederate States to be free. The Proclamation also allowed the Union Army and Navy to enlist Black men. By 1865, around 200,000 Black soldiers and sailors had fought for the Union.

Grant and his generals

Lincoln appointed and dismissed several generals to lead the US army. Meanwhile, the Confederates, under Robert E. Lee, won key battles. Finally, Lincoln appointed Ulysses S. Grant, and the North began to win.

General Grant

Gettysburg Address

In November 1863, Lincoln came to Gettysburg, Pennsylvania, to dedicate a Union cemetery at the site of the deadliest battle of the war. He pledged "that these dead shall not have died in vain".

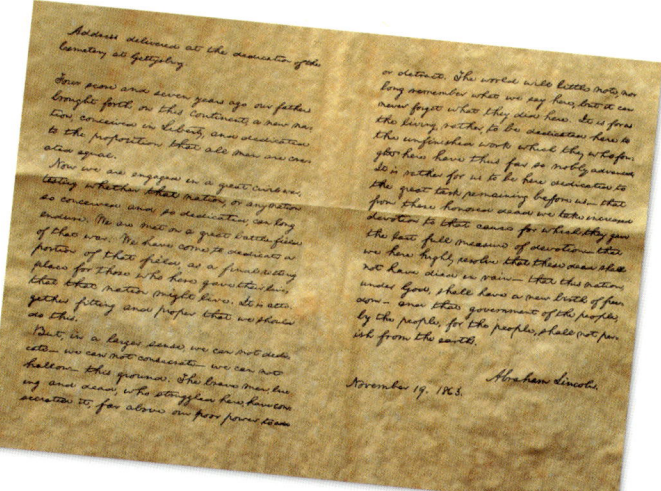

Copy of Lincoln's own draft of the Gettysburg Address

Photograph of Lincoln taken in 1865

Southern general Robert E. Lee

Northern general Ulysses S. Grant

Lee surrenders

On 9 April 1865, Confederate general Robert E. Lee surrendered to Union commander Ulysses S. Grant at Appomattox Court House, Virginia. Lincoln's greatest wish was to secure "a just and lasting peace".

Lincoln is assassinated

On 14 April 1865, Lincoln went to see a play at Ford's Theatre. Confederate sympathizer John Wilkes Booth snuck into Lincoln's box and shot him. Lincoln died the next day, the first president to be killed while in office.

Sheet music for the funeral march

A nation mourns

Thousands of mourners viewed Lincoln's body as it lay in state. He was buried on 4 May 1865, in Springfield, Illinois. The nation had lost a great leader. Lincoln had not believed in punishing the South. With him gone, those bent on revenge gained influence.

Memorial fan

Andrew Johnson

Vest made by Johnson

Tennessee Tailor
Johnson's nickname was the "Tennessee Tailor", as he started his career as a tailor's apprentice. He had no formal schooling and his wife, Eliza, taught him to read and write.

Andrew Johnson was the only Southern US senator to remain loyal to the Union. He was nominated vice president in 1864, and became president after Lincoln's assassination. He tried to enact Lincoln's policy of leniency towards the South following the war, but the "Radical Republicans" resisted. When Johnson refused to yield to their demands, he was impeached.

ANDREW JOHNSON

17TH PRESIDENT
1865–1869

BORN
29 December 1808
Raleigh, North Carolina

INAUGURATED AS PRESIDENT
15 April 1865

AGE AT INAUGURATION
56

PARTY
Democratic

FIRST LADY
Eliza McCardle

CHILDREN
Martha
Charles
Mary
Robert
Andrew

DIED
31 July 1875
Carter County, Tennessee

Johnson in caricature
Even though the Thirteenth Amendment (1865) freed enslaved people, white southerners controlled Black labour through sharecropping and denied them their rights of citizenship. This cartoon shows Johnson as the villainous Iago, from Shakespeare's *Othello*, betraying Othello, who is shown as a Black veteran.

Johnson portrayed as the traitor Iago

This sketch depicts the shooting of Black veterans by police in Memphis in 1866. Over two days, 46 Black people were killed.

Ticket for Johnson's impeachment trial

Impeachment
In 1868, Johnson became the first president to be impeached, or put on trial, by the Senate. There were no constitutional grounds for prosecuting Johnson, just political disagreements over his postwar Reconstruction policies. Although he was spared removal from office by one vote, his presidency was all but over.

Members of the House of Representatives who prosecuted Johnson

Ulysses S Grant

ULYSSES S GRANT

18TH PRESIDENT
1869–1877

BORN
27 April 1822
Point Pleasant, Ohio

INAUGURATED AS PRESIDENT
First term: 4 March 1869
Second term: 4 March 1873

AGE AT INAUGURATION
46

PARTY
Republican

FIRST LADY
Julia Boggs Dent

CHILDREN
Frederick Dent
Ulysses Simpson
Ellen Wrenshall
Jesse Root

DIED
23 July 1885
Mount McGregor, New York

A war hero, Ulysses S Grant became president in 1868, three years after the end of the Civil War. Unfortunately, he was ill-suited to the office, and let dishonest people take advantage of him. After eight years, he was glad to leave office.

General Grant
The Civil War enabled Grant to prove himself. He had been frustrated in several occupations – soldier, farmer, estate agent – before becoming a general. On the battlefield, he was a dynamo.

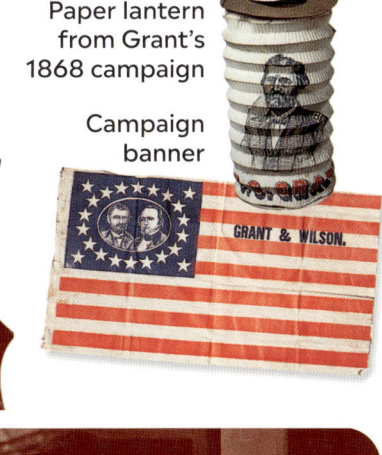

Paper lantern from Grant's 1868 campaign

Campaign banner

Grant was 61 years old when this photograph was taken; he died two years later.

Grant's wife, Julia Boggs Dent

Grant surrounded by his family, 1883

Soldiering on
Grant was unlucky in retirement. In 1884, he lost his savings to an unscrupulous broker. Later, he developed throat cancer. With steely determination, he wrote his memoirs to provide for his family. The book was finished one week before his death. *Personal Memoirs*, written with modesty and humour, was a best seller.

General Grant with his horse during the Civil War

Rutherford B Hayes

Like Ulysses S Grant, Rutherford B Hayes was a Union general in the Civil War. In 1877, he won a controversial election by one electoral college vote. Congress decided the contest, which left many of Hayes's opponents feeling cheated. They referred to Hayes as "His Fraudulency". Hayes proved to be an even-handed, but unexceptional, president. But, by the end of his one term in office, Hayes had won over his critics.

A political bargain
When Samuel J Tilden lost to Hayes, Southern Democrats declared that they would only accept Hayes as president if he removed federal troops from the South.

Great Sioux War
The Black Hills of South Dakota were sacred to the Lakota. When gold was discovered there, Congress tried to remove them. It led to the beginning of the Great Sioux War, which included the Battle of Little Bighorn (right), and lasted between 1876 and 1877. Hayes later signed an act annexing Lakota land.

Lemonade Lucy
Lucy Hayes was the first college-educated first lady. She also backed the temperance movement. The White House banned alcohol, and Lucy was known as "Lemonade Lucy".

Photograph of Lucy Hayes, 1878

Edison telephone, 1879

This bust of Hayes, sculpted in 1876, was intended to convince voters that Hayes was a man of substance.

First phone
Hayes was the first president to use a telephone in the White House.

Chief Tatanka Iyotanka (Sitting Bull) and Tasunke Witco (Crazy Horse) led the Lakota, Arapaho, and Cheyenne warriors.

Ceremonial feather headdress

Little Bighorn River

Former Civil War officer George A Custer leads an attack on the camp of Chief Tatanka Iyotanka in June 1876.

James A Garfield

Garfield was the third Civil War general to become president. The battlefield proved safer than the White House. Four months into his term, Garfield was shot by an assassin. He was the second president to be assassinated while in office.

Memorial ribbon bearing Garfield's portrait

Charles Guiteau
President Garfield

An assassin strikes

President Garfield was shot by Charles Guiteau, who had poor mental health and believed he was owed a federal job. Garfield survived for two months after the shooting. He died on 19 September 1881.

Chester A Arthur

When Garfield was assassinated, Chester A Arthur took on the office. He believed that politicians should earn federal jobs. In 1883, he signed the Pendleton Act, establishing the Civil Service Commission. Job seekers now had to pass exams. The Republican Party did not nominate him for a second term.

Chester A Arthur was a fashionable dresser.

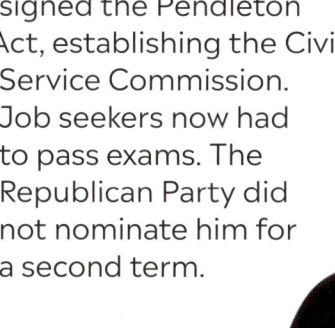

All 200 US soldiers, along with Custer, die in the battle. However, the victory is short-lived for the Lakota.

An illustration from the time depicts a Chinese worker fleeing from a gang of Irish men.

Curb on immigration begins

Economic stagnation in the 1870s led to rising tensions between Chinese and European immigrants competing for jobs in California. Chinese workers faced intense discrimination, and in 1882, the Chinese Exclusion Act was passed to stop immigration from China.

RUTHERFORD B HAYES

19TH PRESIDENT
1877–1881

BORN
4 October 1822
Delaware, Ohio

DIED
17 January 1893
Fremont, Ohio

JAMES A GARFIELD

20TH PRESIDENT
1881

BORN
19 November 1831
Orange Township, Ohio

DIED
19 September 1881
Elberon, New Jersey

CHESTER A ARTHUR

21ST PRESIDENT
1881–1885

BORN
5 October 1830
North Fairfield, Vermont

DIED
18 November 1886
New York, New York

Grover Cleveland

The first Democratic president to be elected after the Civil War, Grover Cleveland was also the first president to serve nonconsecutive terms. He was ousted from office in 1889 by Benjamin Harrison, but returned four years later. Cleveland's second term was plagued by economic depression. Although distressed by the plight of the unemployed, he did not believe in government intervention. He could not restore the economy and had to use federal troops to suppress labour unrest. He failed to win a third nomination.

White House wedding

A highlight of Cleveland's first term was his marriage to Frances Folsom, who, aged 21, became the youngest first lady. Charming and beautiful, Frances was hugely popular, and her image was used in several advertising campaigns.

Sheet music of Cleveland's wedding march

GROVER CLEVELAND

22ND PRESIDENT
1885–1889

24TH PRESIDENT
1893–1897

BORN
18 March 1837
Caldwell, New Jersey

DIED
24 June 1908
Princeton, New Jersey

BENJAMIN HARRISON

23RD PRESIDENT
1889–1893

BORN
20 August 1833
North Bend, Ohio

DIED
13 March 1901
Indianapolis, Indiana

WILLIAM MCKINLEY

25TH PRESIDENT
1897–1901

BORN
29 January 1843, Niles, Ohio

DIED
14 September 1901
Buffalo, New York

Man of destiny

The son of a poor Presbyterian minister, Cleveland received little formal education, but became a successful lawyer. In 1881, he became mayor of Buffalo, New York, where he made his name as a reformer. He was elected governor of New York in 1882 and ran for president in 1884.

Federal troops battle with railway workers.

Pullman rail strike

In 1894, a strike over low pay by workers at the Pullman Palace Car Company led to a railway boycott. Cleveland sent soldiers to break the strike, but the ensuing violence focused public attention on labour rights.

Cleveland campaign banner

Benjamin Harrison

Grandson of William Henry Harrison, the ninth president, Benjamin Harrison was a gifted public speaker, but many people found him aloof. He oversaw the admittance of six new western states to the Union. He also supported the Sherman Antitrust Act of 1890 – designed to eliminate unfair business practices – and the McKinley Tariff Act, which protected businesses from foreign competition. The result was an unpopular rise in prices. Harrison also strengthened the Navy with a view to expanding US influence in Central America and the Pacific.

Immigration
In 1892, the government opened Ellis Island in New York to process the millions of European immigrants arriving in the US. Most immigrants worked in the lowest-paid jobs and suffered hardship. Many were hostile to Harrison for his protection of big business.

Harrison was nicknamed the "Human Iceberg".

William McKinley

Elected in 1896, McKinley favoured a "hands-off" approach to economic affairs. Best remembered for his foreign-policy successes, he helped Cuba win its independence from Spain in 1898. With the Treaty of Paris in 1898, the US acquired Guam, Puerto Rico, and the Philippine islands. That year, it annexed Hawaii. Under McKinley, the nation became a global power.

Pictures of McKinley looking dour give the wrong impression. He was a warm and friendly man who charmed those around him.

McKinley's Republican running mate in the 1900 election campaign was Theodore Roosevelt.

Assassin shoots McKinley
On 6 September 1901, McKinley was shot by anarchist Leon Czolgosz in Buffalo, New York. He died eight days later.

The assassin hid his revolver under a bandage on his hand.

McKinley's inauguration in 1897 was the first to be filmed.

Theodore Roosevelt

In 1901, Theodore Roosevelt became the youngest US president, aged 42. A former writer and cowboy, he had held important political posts and was full of energy and idealism. He wanted a "square deal" for all Americans, which would protect consumer rights, regulate corporations, and conserve natural resources.

THEODORE ROOSEVELT

26TH PRESIDENT
1901–1909

BORN
27 October 1858
New York, New York

INAUGURATED AS PRESIDENT
First term:
14 September 1901
Second term: 4 March 1905

AGE AT INAUGURATION
42

PARTY
Republican

FIRST LADY
Edith Kermit Carow

CHILDREN
Alice Lee
Theodore
Kermit
Ethel Carow
Archibald Bulloch
Quentin

DIED
6 January 1919
Oyster Bay, New York

Inauguration Day

Roosevelt enjoyed his first term as president. He was aware, though, that he had not gained the presidency by election. His popularity was confirmed in 1904 by a solid victory.

Medal celebrating Roosevelt's inauguration in 1904

A Rough Rider

During the Spanish-American War, Roosevelt went to Cuba, which was fighting for independence from Spain. He raised a volunteer cavalry regiment called the Rough Riders and led a charge up San Juan Hill. The Spanish soon surrendered.

The White House Gang

The press nicknamed Roosevelt's young sons the "White House Gang". They had a menagerie of pets and would slide down the central staircase on trays. Daughter Alice enjoyed scandalizing the public. Her father reportedly said: "I can be president ... or I can control Alice. I cannot possibly do both."

President Theodore Roosevelt with his family, 1903

A born rebel, Alice Roosevelt kept a pet snake and liked to smoke in public.

Edith Roosevelt presided over her eccentric family with calm and patience.

Protection for workers

Roosevelt believed that ordinary Americans should be protected against the might of industrialists. When coal miners in Pennsylvania went on strike for higher wages in 1902, he invited both sides to Washington, D.C., for discussions. The miners won many of their demands.

Teddy the crusader

Roosevelt was called the "Trust Buster" for his crusade against businesses that formed trusts to keep prices high and wages low. He used legislation to curb their powers.

This cartoon shows John D Rockefeller, head of the Standard Oil Trust, about to swallow up Earth.

The banner portrays Roosevelt as the protector of labour.

A dinner invitation

Theodore Roosevelt was the first president to invite a Black person to dinner at the White House. This 1901 lithograph celebrates his meeting with Booker T Washington, principal of the Tuskegee Institute in Alabama and a renowned Black educator. However, Roosevelt also held the prevalent view of the time that white people were superior to Black people.

Great outdoorsman

Roosevelt had a passion for the outdoors. He loved to go on hunting trips and safaris. At the time, hunting exotic animals was accepted. As president, he created the first federal game reserves.

Cuddly brown "Teddy's bears", like this one, soon became known as teddy bears and have been beloved by children ever since.

Teddy's bear

According to a popular tale, Roosevelt refused to shoot a captured black bear on a hunting trip. This sketch appeared in *The Washington Post*. "Teddy's bears" were soon being sold as toys.

Once a cowboy

Roosevelt was a sickly boy, and grew to become a believer in strenuous exercise. After the death in 1884 of his first wife, Alice Lee, and his mother on the same day, he became a cowboy in the Dakota Badlands. After two years, he returned to New York, restored.

Roosevelt's leather cowboy chaps

Environmentalism

A farsighted environmentalist, Roosevelt established the first federal wildlife refuge in 1903. By executive order, he preserved millions of hectares of forest and established the first five national parks.

Roosevelt stands with conservationists in front of the "Grizzly Giant" redwood in California.

WILLIAM H. TAFT

27TH PRESIDENT
1909–1913

BORN
15 September 1857
Cincinnati, Ohio

INAUGURATED AS PRESIDENT
4 March 1909

AGE AT INAUGURATION
51

PARTY
Republican

FIRST LADY
Helen (Nellie) Herron

CHILDREN
Robert Alphonso
Helen
Charles Phelps II

DIED
8 March 1930
Washington, D.C.

WOODROW WILSON

28TH PRESIDENT
1913–1921

BORN
28 December 1856
Staunton, Virginia

INAUGURATED AS PRESIDENT
First term: 4 March 1913
Second term: 5 March 1917

AGE AT INAUGURATION
56

PARTY
Democratic

FIRST LADY
Ellen Axson (died 1914)
Edith Bolling Galt

CHILDREN
Margaret Woodrow
Jessie Woodrow
Eleanor Randolph

DIED
3 February 1924
Washington, D.C.

William H Taft

William H Taft was the first and, so far, only president to later serve as Chief Justice of the Supreme Court. His administration followed a progressive agenda, setting up the federal postal savings system and passing the Sixteenth Amendment, which allowed for the collection of personal income tax.

Taft was a good-natured man.

Taft on a diplomatic mission to Japan as Roosevelt's secretary of war, 1905

First ball of the season
As a boy, Taft loved baseball. As president, he decided to throw the first ball on the opening day of baseball season, creating a presidential tradition.

An easygoing manner
Taft was easygoing and gregarious. Yet, after the dynamic Roosevelt, he failed to impress the public. In 1913, he described the White House as "the lonesomest place in the world".

Baseball bat

Catcher's mitt and ball

Despite the jovial appearance on his banners, Taft hated the campaign for election.

A new age arrives
Although Taft kept cows on the White House lawn, he also became the first president to buy a car for the White House.

Early Model T Ford

Woodrow Wilson

Woodrow Wilson was a dynamic reformer, signing legislation to lower tariffs and regulate businesses and banks. He tried hard to keep the US out of World War I, but involvement was inevitable. When the war ended, Wilson helped negotiate the Treaty of Versailles, but the Senate rejected it.

Medal commemorating Wilson's 1913 inauguration

Woodrow Wilson was awarded the Nobel Peace Prize.

The second first lady
Wilson's first wife, Ellen, died during his first term in office. A year later, he was engaged to Edith. After he suffered a stroke in 1919, Edith ran the White House. Many senators were dismayed by having a woman in such a position of power.

A man of principles
A former professor, Wilson found it hard to compromise his moral principles. When the Senate rejected the Treaty of Versailles in 1919, he set off on a national tour to convince people that his ideas were right. Sadly, due to exhaustion, he suffered a stroke three weeks into the tour.

World War I
Despite US neutrality, in 1917 Germany declared that any ships entering the war zone were subject to being fired upon. When Germany also tried to form an anti-American alliance with Mexico, on 2 April 1917, Wilson asked Congress for a declaration of war. The US sent more than a million troops to Europe. They were a decisive factor in the collapse of Germany in October 1918.

World War I recruitment poster of Uncle Sam

President Wilson signing the Treaty of Versailles, 28 June 1919

The Treaty of Versailles
Wilson's Fourteen Points peace plan proposed "peace without victory". However, his European allies did not always agree with his lenient views towards Germany, and he had to accept compromises.

Prohibition
Many people viewed alcohol as the cause of poverty and crime in the US. In 1919, the Volstead Act banned the production, sale, and transport of alcohol. It was the start of Prohibition, a time when illegal "speakeasy" bars and gangsters flourished.

A federal agent nails a "Closed" sign to the door of a bar.

Wilson votes for women
Although Wilson did not initially support the suffragists, he endorsed the Nineteenth Amendment, granting white women the vote. It became law in 1920.

Suffragette button

Warren G. Harding

Harding's campaign theme – "Return to Normalcy" – called for America to return to a simpler way of life after World War I. Unassuming in nature, he yielded much of his executive power to Congress. Unfortunately, Harding delegated authority to dishonest advisers, and scandals sullied his administration. In 1923, before he could be impeached, he died suddenly, sparking rumours that he had been murdered.

Teapot Dome scandal
Secretary of the Interior Albert Fall accepted bribes to allow oil companies to drill in federally protected oil fields near Teapot Dome in Wyoming. He became the first cabinet member sent to prison for crimes committed in office. This event sullied Harding's administration.

Calvin Coolidge

Calvin Coolidge became president upon the death of Harding. Nicknamed "Silent Cal", Coolidge talked little and smiled less. Honest and restrained, Coolidge brought back a sense of trust to the presidency after Harding's administration. The economy was in a period of great prosperity, and he saw no reason to interfere, believing that less government was best.

Straightlaced Cal
Coolidge (centre, with his cabinet, in 1924) was the son of a shopkeeper. A lawyer, he held several political posts before becoming governor of Massachusetts. He was a reserved man, but his upright values served him well in office.

Roaring Twenties
Coolidge's "hands-off" approach to the economy encouraged speculation in the stock market and led to an economic boom. Women found new freedoms: they cut their hair, wore shorter skirts, and went out dancing.

Amazing Grace
Grace Coolidge is pictured here with her tame raccoon, named Rebecca. The first lady was vivacious and enjoyed social gatherings. She was the perfect match for her dour husband. Their happiness was marred, though, when their youngest son died of blood poisoning in 1924.

The story of Lindbergh's Atlantic crossing was celebrated in numerous magazines and books.

The new aviators
In 1926, Coolidge signed the Air Commerce Act to regulate the aviation industry. A year later, Charles Lindbergh made the first non-stop solo flight across the Atlantic. A thrilled Coolidge praised him.

Herbert Hoover

A self-made millionaire, Hoover seemed a perfect choice for president. Unfortunately, only months after he took office, the stock market crashed, triggering the Great Depression. Banks ran out of money, businesses went bust, and people lost their jobs. Many blamed Hoover for the disaster.

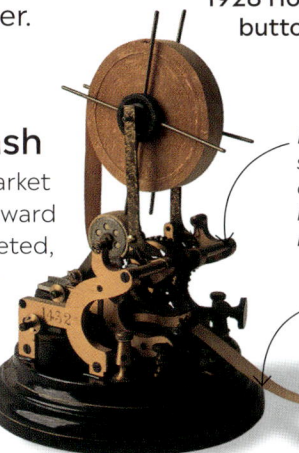

1928 Hoover button

The stock market crash

Fuelled by overspeculation, the stock market crash of 29 October 1929, caused a downward spiral in the economy. Stock prices plummeted, with investors losing $10 billion in just five hours. Many businesses were ruined. The day became known as "Black Tuesday".

News of the stock market collapse came by ticker-tape machine.

Ticker tape

Success story

Despite being orphaned as a child, Hoover became a wealthy mining engineer. Voters of 1928 saw him as an American success story. Four years later, in the midst of the Depression, they had lost faith in him and he was not re-elected.

Button urges voters to re-elect Hoover.

Shantytowns of makeshift homes became known as Hoovervilles.

WARREN G HARDING

29TH PRESIDENT
1921–1923

BORN
2 November 1865
Bloomington Grove, Ohio

DIED
2 August 1923
San Francisco, California

CALVIN COOLIDGE

30TH PRESIDENT
1923–1929

BORN
4 July 1872
Plymouth Notch, Vermont

DIED
5 January 1933
Northampton, Massachusetts

HERBERT HOOVER

31ST PRESIDENT
1929–1933

BORN
10 August 1874
West Branch, Iowa

DIED
20 October 1964
New York, New York

Franklin D Roosevelt

FRANKLIN D ROOSEVELT

32ND PRESIDENT
1933–1945

BORN
30 January 1882
Hyde Park, New York

INAUGURATED AS PRESIDENT
First term: 4 March 1933
Second term: 20 January 1937
Third term: 20 January 1941
Fourth term: 20 January 1945

AGE AT INAUGURATION
51

PARTY
Democratic

FIRST LADY
Anna Eleanor Roosevelt

CHILDREN
Anna Eleanor
James
Franklin Delano, Jr (died in infancy)
Elliott
Franklin Delano, Jr
John Aspinwall

DIED
12 April 1945
Warm Springs, Georgia

KEY EVENTS OF PRESIDENCY

1933 Emergency Banking Act closes the banks; New Deal legislation provides new federal relief programmes.

1939 World War II breaks out.

1940 Roosevelt announces the Lend Lease programme to supply arms to the UK.

1941 Japan attacks Pearl Harbor and the United States enters the war.

1945 Germany and Japan are defeated and World War II ends.

As president during the Great Depression, Roosevelt implemented aid programmes for banks, businesses, farmers, workers, and the unemployed. He empathized with the disadvantaged. Struck by polio in middle age, he could not walk unaided.

Eleanor Roosevelt
Eleanor married Franklin in 1905. She drew attention to the needs of the poor and famously arranged for Black singer Marian Anderson to perform in Washington, D.C., when most entertainment was still segregated.

Like thousands of others, this destitute farm labourer set off on the road with his family to look for work.

The poor and hungry
The effects of the Depression were made worse by a severe drought in the Great Plains, which led the area to become known as the Dust Bowl. Millions suddenly had no work or money. Roosevelt pledged his help.

Pillow cover with anti-Prohibition message

21st Amendment
In 1933, Prohibition ended. The law had led to illicit bootlegging, smuggling, and the rise of gangsters.

Sheet music for the rousing New Deal March

A New Deal for all
Roosevelt called his programme of aid and reform the New Deal. One of his goals was to put people back to work. He wanted to help what he called the forgotten man – the ordinary worker who was unemployed and hungry. He established federal programmes for financial aid and work projects – solutions that Hoover had refused to consider.

Roosevelt talks to the nation
After the 1933 banking collapse, the president said, "The only thing we have to fear is fear itself", and temporarily closed the banks. In his first radio "fireside chat", he urged people to put their cash back into the banks. They did.

First friend
Roosevelt's black Scottie dog, Fala, accompanied the president everywhere and soon became a national celebrity.

Reassuring radio broadcasts became an important aspect of Roosevelt's appeal.

In the 1930s, radio was the fastest way of communicating important news to the nation.

Dr Win-the-War

In 1940, Roosevelt won a historic third term. While still dealing with the Depression, he was faced with another crisis – World War II. The US entered the war in December 1941, after Japan attacked the US naval base at Pearl Harbor. With the Allied leaders Winston Churchill of the UK and Joseph Stalin of the Soviet Union, Roosevelt planned strategies to defeat Germany, Italy, and Japan. In 1944, he won re-election, but the war had taken its toll on his health. He died in April 1945, a month before Germany surrendered.

In 1943, Roosevelt stated that "Dr New Deal" had to become "Dr Win-the-War".

USS Shaw explodes as it is hit by a Japanese bomb in Pearl Harbor.

Pearl Harbor

On 7 December 1941, Japanese bombers carried out a surprise attack on US bases at Pearl Harbor, Hawaii. More than 2,300 servicemen were killed, 1,300 wounded, and 1,000 unaccounted for. Calling the attack "a date which will live in infamy", the president led the US into World War II.

The Manhattan Project

In 1939, Roosevelt heard from German scientist Albert Einstein (left) that Germany might be developing an atomic bomb. He allocated $2 billion to the "Manhattan Project" at Columbia University in Manhattan, led by American physicist J Robert Oppenheimer. On 16 July 1945, the US detonated the world's first atomic bomb in the New Mexico desert.

The home front

When the US entered the war, millions were needed to serve in the armed forces. At home, this left many jobs unfilled. The government launched campaigns urging Americans to join the war effort. Roosevelt put his energy into getting factories to retool for war production.

This poster contains the words of one of Roosevelt's morale-boosting speeches.

With so many men overseas, it became more socially acceptable for women to work outside the home.

The American flag was raised by Marines over the Pacific island of Iwo Jima after one of the hardest-fought battles of the war.

This statue in Arlington is based on a 1945 photo by Joe Rosenthal. It shows the bravery and sacrifice of US Marines in World War II.

The Big Three at Tehran, Iran, in November 1943 — Joseph Stalin, Franklin D Roosevelt, Winston Churchill

The Big Three

In November 1943, Roosevelt met with Churchill and Stalin. The "Big Three" discussed plans for a joint invasion of German-occupied France. The D-Day invasion took place on 6 June 1944. Headed by General Dwight Eisenhower, it led to the liberation of France and German defeat.

Many believed Roosevelt should not run for a fourth term. This campaign item stressed that he should continue.

Victory in the Pacific

In February 1945, almost 7,000 US soldiers were lost in a four-day battle at Iwo Jima in the Pacific. Japan eventually surrendered to the US on 14 August 1945.

Harry S Truman

HARRY S TRUMAN

33RD PRESIDENT
1945–1953

BORN
8 May 1884
Lamar, Missouri

INAUGURATED AS PRESIDENT
First term: 12 April 1945
Second term: 20 January 1949

AGE AT INAUGURATION
60

PARTY
Democratic

FIRST LADY
Elizabeth (Bess) Virginia Wallace

CHILDREN
Margaret

DIED
26 December 1972
Kansas City, Missouri

Roosevelt's death in 1945 put Truman in the White House. The war in Europe was ending, but the Pacific war dragged on. The Japanese refused to surrender, and Truman did not want to risk more US lives. He ordered two atomic bombs to be dropped on Japan. Within days, the war was over. After the war, his "Fair Deal" bills proposed national medical insurance and a civil rights bill, but both were defeated in Congress.

The Trumans at home
Although he met his future wife at Sunday school at age six, Truman and "Bess" Wallace did not marry until 1919, when they were in their thirties. Here, Truman is seen in a cheery mood with his wife (left) and daughter, Margaret (right), giving information for a census.

Man from Independence
Roosevelt was a hard act to follow. Truman, a plain-spoken former haberdasher from Independence, Missouri, often appeared brash in comparison. One of his favourite sayings was, "If you can't stand the heat, get out of the kitchen".

Atomic bomb
On 6 August 1945, the US bomber *Enola Gay* dropped an atomic bomb over Hiroshima, killing at least 100,000 people. Truman wrote, "We have discovered the most terrible bomb in the history of the world".

A mushroom-shaped cloud of smoke and dust rose 8 km (5 miles) above Hiroshima.

The Truman Doctrine

After the war, Soviet leader Stalin established communist regimes in Eastern Europe. The US supported capitalism and worried about the spread of communism. In 1947, the Truman Doctrine aimed to contain communism, and Secretary of State George Marshall proposed the Marshall Plan to help war-torn Europe. Stalin denounced the aid as a capitalist plot. The Cold War had begun.

Airlift

In April 1948, the USSR blockaded Berlin, Germany, to end the Allied presence in the city. Truman ordered supplies to be airlifted to Berlin. US and British supply planes helped Berliners to survive until the blockade was lifted in May 1949.

Children in Berlin watch as an airplane brings in vital supplies.

The Korean War

When communist North Korea invaded South Korea in 1950, the fear of the spread of communism led Truman to send US troops to the other side of the world. General Douglas MacArthur had orders to liberate South Korea. His invasion worried neighbouring China, which sent vast numbers of troops. The war lasted until 1953.

US troops on the move in Korea

Dwight D Eisenhower

Eisenhower's presidency was largely peaceful and prosperous for many. He ended the Korean War in 1953 and tried to improve relations with the USSR by organizing cultural exchanges. These ended when a US spy plane was shot down in Soviet airspace.

Likable Ike
"I Like Ike" was one of the most memorable campaign slogans of the 1950s. Eisenhower won a landslide victory in the 1952 election.

"I Like Ike" buttons were worn everywhere – even by those who usually voted Democrat.

Popular first lady
Mamie's image as a wife and mother whose main concerns were home and entertaining was used to promote her husband as a family man.

A 1956 campaign bucket for Eisenhower and running mate Richard Nixon

DWIGHT D EISENHOWER

34TH PRESIDENT
1953–1961

BORN
14 October 1890
Denison, Texas

INAUGURATED AS PRESIDENT
First term:
20 January 1953
Second term:
21 January 1957

AGE AT INAUGURATION
62

PARTY
Republican

DIED
28 March 1969
Washington, D.C.

Mamie frequently wore pink and even decorated the White House in this colour.

Avid golfer
Eisenhower loved to play golf. He had a putting green and driving range built on the White House grounds, and was often seen there practicing his swing.

These "Ike" golf tees from the 1956 Republican campaign promoted the president through his favourite sport.

Eisenhower shakes hands with his five-year-old grandson David on a Georgia golf course.

The McCarthy hearings
In the 1950s, the US feared communist infiltration. Senator Joseph McCarthy of Wisconsin became notorious for his communist "witch hunts" in the State Department. His allegations ruined innocent people. Ultimately, he was ruined by his own slanders.

Senator McCarthy chuckles over an anti-McCarthyist advertisement in 1954.

Elizabeth Eckford faces an angry mob as she tries to attend her first day of school.

World War II general
Eisenhower had a distinguished military career. In World War II, he led the European Theatre of Operations. After invading North Africa and Italy, he was made Supreme Allied Commander in Europe and organized the D-Day landings. After the war, he became chief of staff, the army's highest office.

Eisenhower in his World War II general's uniform

Little Rock
In 1954, the Supreme Court ruled that segregating Black and white citizens was illegal. In the South, however, there was strong resistance. In 1957, Governor Faubus of Little Rock, Arkansas, tried to prevent Black students from enrolling in an all-white high school. Eisenhower sent 1,000 federal troops of the 101st Airborne Division to escort the students safely to school.

Sputnik I

The Space Race
On 4 October 1957, the USSR launched the first satellite, *Sputnik I*, into space. Until then, US scientists had believed their space technology to be ahead of the Russians'. With Eisenhower's approval, Congress set up NASA. The Space Race had begun.

47

John F Kennedy

At 43, John F Kennedy was the youngest president ever elected, bringing a sense of possibility to the White House. He fought for civil rights legislation to ensure equal rights for all, regardless of race. In 1961, he challenged the Soviet Union to put a man on the Moon by the end of the decade. However, his term of office was tragically brief; Kennedy was assassinated in 1963.

First lady of style
Jacqueline Bouvier married John Kennedy in 1953. Stylish and charismatic, "Jackie" brought glamour to the White House and refurbished many of its rooms.

Commemorative badge

Portrait of a president
Kennedy was born on 29 May 1917, into a large Irish-Catholic family. His father was millionaire tycoon Joseph P Kennedy. After graduating from Harvard University in 1940, "Jack" joined the Navy. During World War II, he was decorated for heroism.

Electioneering
Kennedy enjoyed politicking and, in 1960, ran for president with typical enthusiasm. He flew around the US in his own airplane, wooing voters with his charm.

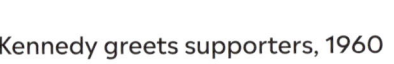

Kennedy greets supporters, 1960

Fidel Castro of Cuba
Nikita Khrushchev

Cuban Missile Crisis
When Soviet nuclear missile sites were found in Cuba, Kennedy ordered a blockade of the island. In 1962, the US and USSR teetered on the brink of war for 13 days. Soviet premier Khrushchev backed down after a secret deal was reached.

"I have a dream"
In August 1963, Martin Luther King, Jr, delivered his now-famous speech in Washington, D.C. He invoked the Declaration of Independence, saying: "I have a dream that one day this nation will rise up and live out the true meaning of its creed: 'We hold these truths to be self-evident, that all men are created equal.'"

Martin Luther King, Jr's policy of nonviolence attracted huge numbers of supporters to his cause.

President killed in Dallas, Texas
On 22 November 1963, Kennedy was riding through Dallas when an assassin opened fire. He was hit in the head and killed. Police arrested 24-year-old Lee Harvey Oswald, who was shot two days later by Jack Ruby while in police custody.

This photograph of John F Kennedy was taken moments before he was fatally shot.

JOHN F KENNEDY

35TH PRESIDENT
1961–1963

BORN
29 May 1917
Brookline, Massachusetts

INAUGURATED AS PRESIDENT
20 January 1961

AGE AT INAUGURATION
43

PARTY
Democratic

FIRST LADY
Jacqueline Lee Bouvier

CHILDREN
Caroline Bouvier
John Fitzgerald, Jr
Patrick Bouvier

DIED
22 November 1963
Dallas, Texas

Jackie Kennedy's quiet dignity at her husband's funeral moved the hearts of millions of television viewers.

John Connally, governor of Texas, was also wounded in the shooting.

Jackie Kennedy was not injured.

America mourns
A grieving nation watched the televised burial of John F Kennedy at Arlington National Cemetery, Virginia, on 25 November 1963. Representatives of 93 nations came to pay their respects. Kennedy was president for just 1,037 days.

Lyndon B Johnson

Lady Bird Johnson (left) and Jackie Kennedy (right) look on as Lyndon B Johnson is sworn in as president within hours of JFK's death.

Lyndon B Johnson became president after the tragic death of John F Kennedy. A tall Texan, "LBJ" declared a "war on poverty" and tried to promote racial harmony, although race riots flared up, as did protests against the Vietnam War. A disheartened Johnson chose not to seek re-election.

Johnson's dream

Johnson dreamed of a "Great Society", free of racial hatred and poverty. His programme of social legislation included the Civil Rights Act of 1964, which banned racial segregation in public places and employment discrimination, and the Voting Rights Act of 1965, which outlawed the literacy requirement for voters.

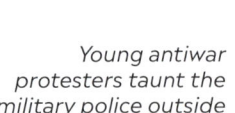

The LBJ family

It was a family tradition that all the Johnsons had the initials "LBJ". Johnson's dog was Little Beagle Johnson. His children were Lynda Bird and Luci Baines, and the first lady was nicknamed Lady Bird. Her real name was Claudia Alta.

Sheet music for the Great Society March

ALL AMERICANS MOVE FORWARD

"We have talked long enough in this country about equal rights. We have talked 100 years or more. It is time to write the next chapter, and write it in the books of law."

—President Johnson
November 27, 1963

Poster promoting Johnson's stand on civil rights

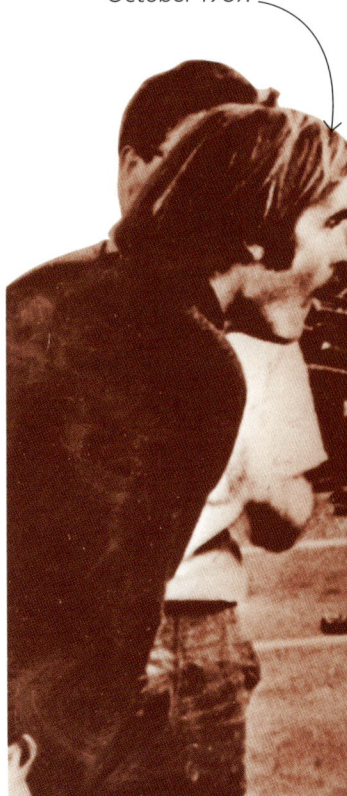

Young antiwar protesters taunt the military police outside the Pentagon in October 1967.

The first US combat troops land at Da Nang, South Vietnam, 11 March 1965.

LYNDON B JOHNSON

36TH PRESIDENT
1963–1969

BORN
27 August 1908
Near Stonewall, Texas

INAUGURATED AS PRESIDENT
First term: 22 Nov 1963
Second term: 20 Jan 1965

AGE AT INAUGURATION
55

PARTY
Democratic

FIRST LADY
Claudia Alta Taylor

CHILDREN
Lynda Bird
Luci Baines

DIED
22 January 1973
San Antonio, Texas

The Vietnam War

When Johnson became president, about 16,000 US soldiers were in South Vietnam trying to stop the communists in the North from taking over the entire country. In 1965, he ordered bombing raids and sent troops to protect US bases. By 1968, the US had more than 500,000 troops in Vietnam. With no victory in sight and casualties mounting, Johnson despaired of finding a quick and honourable end to the war.

Antiwar poster of a battered Uncle Sam

Peace protests

Antiwar protests gave rise to the Sixties' counterculture of hippies and "flower children". The Vietnam War cost Johnson dearly. Voted "Man of the Year" by *Time* magazine in 1964, by 1968, he was reviled.

Around **100,000 antiwar protesters** gathered at the Lincoln Memorial on 21 October 1967.

Richard M Nixon

An able vice president to Eisenhower from 1953 to 1961, Richard M Nixon lost a tight presidential race to Kennedy in 1960. Just as his political career seemed over, he was elected president in 1968. He had a flair for foreign diplomacy, witnessed the lunar landing, and brought an end to US involvement in Vietnam. Yet, he is best known for the Watergate scandal. He is the only president to resign.

On his way up
After failing to win the presidency, Nixon left politics in 1962 to practice law. Before long, he was the Republican candidate in the 1968 election.

Nixon inaugural pennants

Early days
The son of a grocer, Nixon practiced law before joining the Navy in 1942. Elected to Congress in 1946, he was nicknamed "Tricky Dick" for his cunning in politics.

A match for Mao
Sensing a rift between America's Cold War enemies China and the Soviet Union, Nixon opened negotiations with Chairman Mao. In 1971, Mao invited the US Ping-Pong team to China, and Nixon met with Chinese premier Zhou Enlai. In 1972, he continued this policy of *détente*, or relaxation, by visiting Moscow.

Mao and Nixon hit a Ping-Pong ball, and opposing ideologies, in this cartoon.

Artist Norman Rockwell said Nixon was "the hardest man" he ever painted.

Buzz Aldrin photographed on the Moon's surface by Neil Armstrong

"The Eagle has landed"
On 20 July 1969, the US put a man on the Moon, fulfilling JFK's 1961 pledge. President Nixon spoke with astronauts Neil Armstrong and Edwin "Buzz" Aldrin during their Moon walk. Millions worldwide watched the event on television.

RICHARD NIXON

37TH PRESIDENT
1969–1974

BORN
9 January 1913
Yorba Linda, California

INAUGURATED AS PRESIDENT
First term:
20 January 1969
Second term:
20 January 1973

AGE AT INAUGURATION
56

PARTY
Republican

FIRST LADY
Thelma Catherine (Pat) Ryan

CHILDREN
Patricia
Julie

DIED
22 April 1994
New York, New York

Nixon shakes hands with GIs during his tour of Vietnam in July 1969.

Watergate
In June 1972, burglars were found planting bugging devices in the Democratic Party headquarters at the Watergate complex in Washington, D.C. Nixon denied involvement, but witnesses testified that he had ordered a cover-up of the scandal, and had taped all conversations held in the Oval Office. After the tapes were heard in July 1974, Nixon faced impeachment.

Vietnam
To bring an end to the Vietnam War, Nixon decided on a policy of "Vietnamization". This meant replacing US combat forces with South Vietnamese troops. The US signed a peace agreement with North Vietnam in January 1973. By March, all US combat troops had been withdrawn.

Nixon resigns
In a press conference in November 1973, Nixon declared, "I am not a crook". Yet, it soon became clear that Nixon had been involved in illegal activities. In August 1974, he was forced to resign or face impeachment. On leaving the White House on 9 August, Nixon forced a grin and gave his usual victory salute.

Nixon makes his resignation speech.

Gerald R Ford

Gerald R Ford was the first president to hold office without having been elected. Appointed vice president by Nixon after the elected vice president, Spiro Agnew, stepped down in 1973, Ford was sworn in as president in 1974 when Nixon resigned. In a controversial gesture to heal the nation, he pardoned Nixon. He also gave amnesty to Vietnam deserters and draft-dodgers.

An eventful year
A highlight of Ford's two-and-a-half-year presidency was the 1976 Bicentennial celebration of the nation's founding. Later that year, Ford lost the presidential election to Jimmy Carter.

In 1934, **Gerald Ford** was selected the Most **Valuable Player** for the Michigan Wolverines, his college football team.

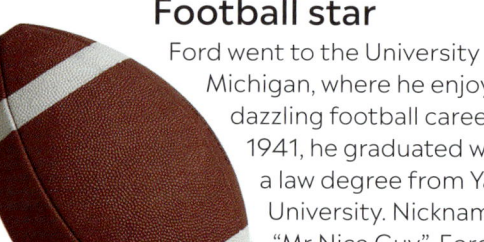

Football star
Ford went to the University of Michigan, where he enjoyed a dazzling football career. In 1941, he graduated with a law degree from Yale University. Nicknamed "Mr Nice Guy", Ford had a reputation for being a patient thinker.

GERALD R FORD

38TH PRESIDENT
1974–1977

BORN
14 July 1913
Omaha, Nebraska

INAUGURATED AS PRESIDENT
9 August 1974

AGE AT INAUGURATION
61

PARTY
Republican

FIRST LADY
Elizabeth Anne Bloomer

CHILDREN
Michael Gerald
John Gardner
Steven Meigs
Susan Elizabeth

DIED
26 December 2006
Rancho Mirage, California

President Ford with his wife Betty and their family

A brave first lady
Betty Ford was a charismatic and outspoken first lady. She was a champion of women's rights and those of children with disabilities. After her husband left office, Mrs Ford bravely admitted to being an alcoholic and dependent on prescription drugs. With treatment, she recovered and went on to help found the Betty Ford Center in California.

Evacuation of Saigon
The peace treaty negotiated by Nixon in Vietnam did not last long. In April 1975, communist forces captured the city of Saigon in South Vietnam. Prior to the invasion, hundreds of US citizens and Vietnamese refugees were airlifted to safety.

Jimmy Carter

When Americans voted for Jimmy Carter, they were voting for change. People were tired of scandal-ridden politics and high inflation. But improving the economy proved harder than Carter had predicted. Nor could he ease the energy crisis. Americans soon regarded him as ineffective.

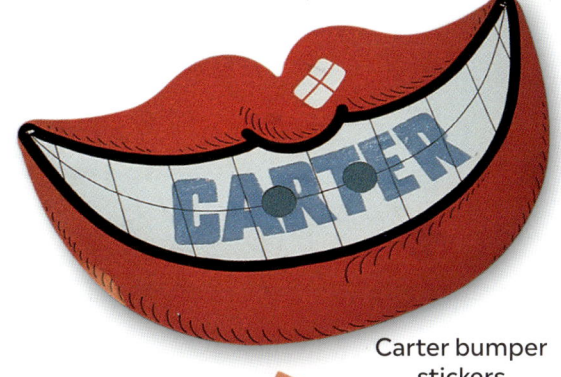

Carter bumper stickers

Peanut farmer
Carter grew up on a peanut farm in Georgia. After studying nuclear physics, he joined the Navy. When his father died, Carter returned to run the family business.

JIMMY CARTER

39TH PRESIDENT
1977–1981

BORN
1 October 1924
Plains, Georgia

INAUGURATED AS PRESIDENT
20 January 1977

AGE AT INAUGURATION
53

PARTY
Democratic

FIRST LADY
Eleanor Rosalynn Smith

CHILDREN
John William, James Earl III, Donnel Jeffrey, Amy Lynn

DIED
29 December 2024
Plains, Georgia

Carter delivers Camp David Accords
In 1978, Carter hosted peace talks between President Sadat of Egypt and Prime Minister Begin of Israel at Camp David, Maryland. The accords they signed ended the state of war between the two countries that had existed since 1948.

Carter grapples with Iran
In November 1979, militant Iranians took the staff of the US embassy in Tehran hostage. They were angered by US support of the exiled shah of Iran. Carter's negotiations for the hostages' release failed, as did a military rescue mission in April 1980. The stalemate made him look weak and shattered his re-election chances. The hostages were released in January 1981, minutes after Reagan took office.

Ronald Reagan

A former actor, Ronald Reagan was called the "Great Communicator" because of his ease on camera. His economic plan, Reaganomics, included reducing taxes for the rich, and cutting welfare programs in the since-disproven belief that it would "trickle down". The Reagan Doctrine, which aimed to reverse communism, helped end the Cold War.

Star quality
The son of a shoe salesman, Reagan started his career as a radio announcer. In 1937, he went to Hollywood, where he acted in more than 50 films, including the 1951 *Bedtime for Bonzo*, above.

1984 campaign belt buckle

Painting of Reagan by Aaron Shikler that appeared on the cover of *Time* magazine in January 1981

Assassination attempt
Shortly after he took office in 1981, President Reagan was shot. As doctors prepared to remove a bullet from his lung, the president joked, "I forgot to duck". Reagan made a remarkable recovery.

Reagan and Gorbachev pose for photographers in 1986.

Cold War thaw
When Mikhail Gorbachev became leader of the Soviet Union in 1985, he embarked on arms-control talks with Reagan. In 1988, they signed the Intermediate Range Nuclear Forces Treaty.

Nancy Reagan

Nancy Reagan was a former actor, who used the stage name Nancy Davis. She became Reagan's second wife in 1952. Although a popular first lady, she was criticized for her lavish tastes and for having too much influence on Reagan's political career.

Nancy launched a campaign to warn young people against drug abuse.

Moments after this photo was taken, the Challenger space shuttle exploded.

Shuttle disaster

The US space programme suffered a huge setback when the *Challenger* space shuttle exploded shortly after liftoff on 28 January 1986. All seven astronauts were killed. The "Star Wars" defence system also received bad publicity. It was meant to divert nuclear missiles away from the US using space-based lasers, but years of costly research produced little.

Lieutenant Colonel Oliver North arranged the money transfers to the Contras. Here, he testifies before Congress.

The Iran-Contra Affair

In 1986, it was revealed that the National Security Council had illegally sold weapons to Iran. Money from the arms deals was used to aid the anticommunist guerrilla group Contra in Nicaragua. Reagan claimed he knew nothing of the deals, but his credibility suffered.

RONALD REAGAN

40TH PRESIDENT
1981–1989

BORN
6 February 1911
Tampico, Illinois

INAUGURATED AS PRESIDENT
First term:
20 January 1981
Second term:
20 January 1985

AGE AT INAUGURATION
69

PARTY
Republican

FIRST LADY
Nancy Davis

CHILDREN
Maureen Elizabeth, Michael Edward, Patti Davis, Ronald Prescott

DIED
5 June 2004
Los Angeles, California

George H W Bush

Foreign affairs dominated George H W Bush's presidency. In 1989, he sent troops into Panama to oust former ally Manuel Noriega. A year later, he rallied a multinational coalition to force Iraq out of oil-rich Kuwait. Yet, as the country went into recession, Bush's popularity eroded, especially after he raised taxes despite saying "Read my lips, no new taxes" during his campaign.

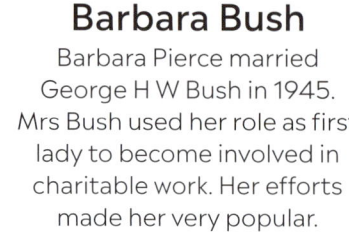

Barbara Bush
Barbara Pierce married George H W Bush in 1945. Mrs Bush used her role as first lady to become involved in charitable work. Her efforts made her very popular.

Win one, lose one
Bush was the first sitting vice president to be elected president since 1836. But when he ran for re-election, he could not convince voters to stick with his conservative agenda.

Bush was Ronald Reagan's running mate in 1980 and 1984.

President Bush cheers on US troops during the Gulf War.

Saving the planet
In his 1988 campaign, Bush promised to be the environmental president. In 1992, at the United Nations Earth Summit, he signed the Earth Pledge, requiring nations to limit the emission of greenhouse gases, monitor biodiversity, and work towards eco-friendly development. But he would not increase financial aid to support the environmental goals of developing nations.

East rejoins West at last
On 9 November 1989, East Germans began to tear down the Berlin Wall, which had stood for 28 years. This marked the end of the Cold War. By 1990, Germany was reunified and communist governments in Eastern Europe began to collapse. There was now a "new world order".

Germans from East and West join hands along the Berlin Wall in front of the Brandenburg Gate.

The Gulf War
In August 1990, Iraq's leader, Saddam Hussein, ordered the invasion of oil-rich Kuwait. Bush coordinated a military coalition of US and allied forces to regain control of Kuwait and its oil. In January 1991, the bombing campaign Operation Desert Storm was launched against Iraq. Six weeks later, the Iraqis were driven out of Kuwait.

GEORGE H W BUSH

41ST PRESIDENT
1989–1993

BORN
12 June 1924
Milton, Massachusetts

INAUGURATED AS PRESIDENT
20 January 1989

AGE AT INAUGURATION
64

PARTY
Republican

FIRST LADY
Barbara Pierce

CHILDREN
George Walker
Robin
John Ellis "Jeb"
Neil Mallon
Marvin Pierce
Dorothy

DIED
30 November 2018
Houston, Texas

Bill Clinton

The first US president to be born after World War II, Bill Clinton knew early on that he wanted to hold high office. As president, he enjoyed the longest period of economic expansion in the US during peacetime. In his first term, he signed NAFTA (North American Free Trade Agreement), negotiated by George H W Bush, into law and also restored peace and democracy in Haiti. Congress, however, refused to pass his health-care reforms. His second term was marred by scandal, but even this did not diminish his popularity.

1996 commemorative campaign item

BILL CLINTON

42ND PRESIDENT
1993–2001

BORN
19 August 1946
Hope, Arkansas

INAUGURATED AS PRESIDENT
First term: 20 January 1993
Second term:
20 January 1997

AGE AT INAUGURATION
46

PARTY
Democratic

FIRST LADY
Hillary Rodham

CHILDREN
Chelsea

Clinton with his wife Hillary and daughter Chelsea

The first family
Bill Clinton and Hillary Rodham first met at Yale University Law School. They married in 1975 and moved to Little Rock, Arkansas, in 1976, when Clinton was appointed state attorney general. They have one child, Chelsea, who was born in 1980.

A second term
Clinton and running mate Al Gore were re-elected for a second term in 1996.

A fateful encounter
In 1963, 16-year-old Bill visited the White House as part of a national conference of high school students. He shook hands with his hero, JFK. The encounter fuelled his ambition to become president.

Foreign affairs
In 1999, Clinton agreed to support NATO (North Atlantic Treaty Organization) air strikes against Serbia to prevent ethnic cleansing in Kosovo (above). Part of the former Yugoslavia, Kosovo was inhabited mainly by ethnic Albanians, who were forced to flee as Serbian soldiers invaded. The bombing forced the Serbs into submission. Kosovo declared independence in 2008.

Political family
No first lady has been as active in politics as Hillary Clinton. In 2000, she became a US senator. She campaigned for the presidency in 2008, but lost the Democratic bid to Barack Obama. In 2016, she became the first woman to be nominated for president, but lost the election to Donald Trump.

Clinton confesses
In 1998, Clinton faced allegations about a relationship with a 21-year-old White House intern, Monica Lewinsky. He initially denied the allegations, but later admitted to a grand jury that he had an "inappropriate relationship" with her. Impeachment proceedings on charges of lying under oath and obstruction of justice followed in January 1999. Clinton was acquitted.

Clinton gathers his thoughts before making a personal statement to the nation concerning his relationship with Monica Lewinsky.

Clinton waits in the Map Room of the White House, 17 August 1998.

Pin in the shape of Clinton's saxophone

Campaign button reads: "The cure for the blues".

Rhythm and Blues
A talented musician, Bill Clinton was offered music scholarships after high school. Instead, he studied politics at Georgetown University in Washington, D.C. As president, he, on occasion, played his sax for the public.

George W Bush

Like John Quincy Adams, George W Bush was the son of a former president. Following the terrorist attacks of 11 September 2001, Bush launched a "war on terror". He sent troops to Afghanistan to hunt for militant leader Osama bin Laden and to overthrow the Taliban, the brutal group that ruled Afghanistan and protected Al-Qaeda. In 2003, he targeted the regime of Iraqi dictator Saddam Hussein. The unpopular war dominated his second term.

President "W"
To distinguish him from his father, the younger Bush was called "W". While the nickname was used affectionately by those who approved of his time in office, detractors pronounced it "Dubya" disapprovingly.

Commemorative campaign toys

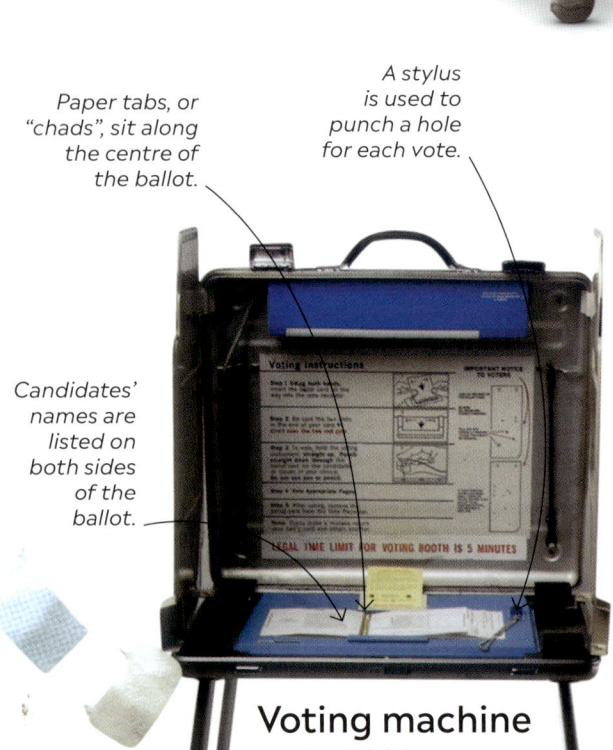

Paper tabs, or "chads", sit along the centre of the ballot.

A stylus is used to punch a hole for each vote.

Candidates' names are listed on both sides of the ballot.

Voting machine
In the 2000 election, ballots in Florida were miscounted by machines. Reviewers had to recount votes by hand to decide if a partial punch or "hanging chad" represented an intentional vote.

The campaign trail
Bush had to defeat the popular John McCain for the Republican nomination, then battle Vice President Al Gore. He won a slim majority of the Electoral College vote, but not the popular vote. The fight over alleged miscounts in Florida went to the Supreme Court. He was declared the winner weeks after election day.

September 11 (9/11)

On 11 September 2001, the Middle Eastern terrorist group Al-Qaeda hijacked airplanes to use as missiles. Two planes destroyed the World Trade Center in Manhattan – one damaged the Pentagon in Virginia and one crashed in Pennsylvania. More than 3,000 people were killed in the attacks.

GEORGE W BUSH

43RD PRESIDENT
2001–2009

BORN
6 July 1946
New Haven, Connecticut

INAUGURATED AS PRESIDENT
First term: 20 January 2001
Second term: 20 January 2005

AGE AT INAUGURATION
54

PARTY
Republican

FIRST LADY
Laura Welch

CHILDREN
Barbara, Jenna

Bullhorn used to address workers
Gas mask to protect from smoke and ash

World Trade Center
New York City saw the greatest loss of life from the 9/11 attacks with the fall of the World Trade Center's twin towers. Firefighters, police, and civilian volunteers worked around the clock to clear the site in Lower Manhattan. Bush made several visits to the area to show support.

The Iraq War
Bush ordered the invasion of Iraq on 20 March 2003 to oust its leader, Saddam Hussein. His administration asserted that Iraq had weapons of mass destruction, a claim later comprehensively discredited. Ultimately, tens of thousands of people died in the war, and Hussein was executed by the Iraqi government for crimes against humanity.

Mission accomplished?
On 1 May 2003, President Bush visited the aircraft carrier USS *Abraham Lincoln* to announce the major combat mission in the Iraq War had ended. However, the war continued for eight more years.

A long war
US soldiers remained in Iraq for almost 20 years. As many as half a million people are believed to have died in the conflict and the insurgency and civil war that followed.

Barack Obama

A Hawaii native, Barack Obama was the first president not to be born on the mainland. Born to a Kenyan father and an American mother, he was the country's first biracial leader. As president, his signature achievement was winning a long fight to establish the Affordable Care Act. He was re-elected in 2012 to serve a second term.

An unconventional childhood
Obama's parents divorced, and young Barack was raised by his mother and grandparents in Hawaii and Indonesia.

Organizing the community
After graduating from Columbia University in 1983, Obama became a community organizer in a public housing development. He faced many challenges to help the low-income residents he represented. The experience prepared him for work as a civil rights lawyer and US senator.

Rivalry within the party
Barack Obama and Hillary Clinton were neck-and-neck in the 2008 Democratic primaries. Clinton lost by a narrow margin and went on to support Obama. She later became Secretary of State in his cabinet.

BARACK H OBAMA

44TH PRESIDENT
2009–2017

BORN
4 August 1961
Honolulu, Hawaii

INAUGURATED AS PRESIDENT
First term: 20 January 2009
Second term:
21 January 2013

AGE AT INAUGURATION
47

PARTY
Democratic

FIRST LADY
Michelle Robinson

CHILDREN
Malia, Sasha

Literary legacy
Obama wrote a memoir called *Dreams from My Father* and a political book called *The Audacity of Hope*, which became a best seller. He has also written the first volume of his presidential memoir, *A Promised Land*.

First Lady Michelle Obama
The first Black first lady, Michelle Obama became a global role model for women. She championed the right of girls to receive a proper education and ran a campaign to reduce childhood obesity.

"Yes We Can"
As a candidate with a message of hope and change, Obama used the slogan "Yes We Can" in his 2008 presidential run. His 2012 message was "Forward 2012".

Obamamania
In 2004, Obama delivered the keynote address at the Democratic National Convention and became a political superstar. Young and eloquent, he appealed to a new generation of voters. His image was featured on magazines, advertising hoardings, and T-shirts.

Obama's mural in New York City by US artist Shepard Fairey

The Affordable Care Act
In his first term, Obama signed into law his health-care reform to cut the high cost of health care. The Affordable Care Act – dubbed "Obamacare" – was challenged by opponents, but upheld by the Supreme Court.

The first family
Obama met his wife, Michelle, while working at a Chicago law firm. They married in 1992 and have two daughters, Malia and Sasha.

Donald Trump

DONALD TRUMP

45TH PRESIDENT
2017-2021

47TH PRESIDENT
2025-

BORN
14 June 1946
Queens, New York

INAUGURATED AS PRESIDENT
First term: 20 January 2017
Second term:
20 January 2025

AGE AT INAUGURATION
70 / 78

PARTY
Republican

FIRST LADY
Melania Trump

CHILDREN
Donald Jr.
Ivanka
Eric
Tiffany
Barron

Elected under the slogan "Make America Great Again" in 2017, Donald Trump found popularity with voters who felt left behind by globalization and elected officials. Trump was impeached twice by the House of Representatives, but was acquitted by the Senate. After losing in the 2020 election, in 2024, he won a second term defeating the Democrat candidate Kamala Harris, and became the oldest person to be elected president.

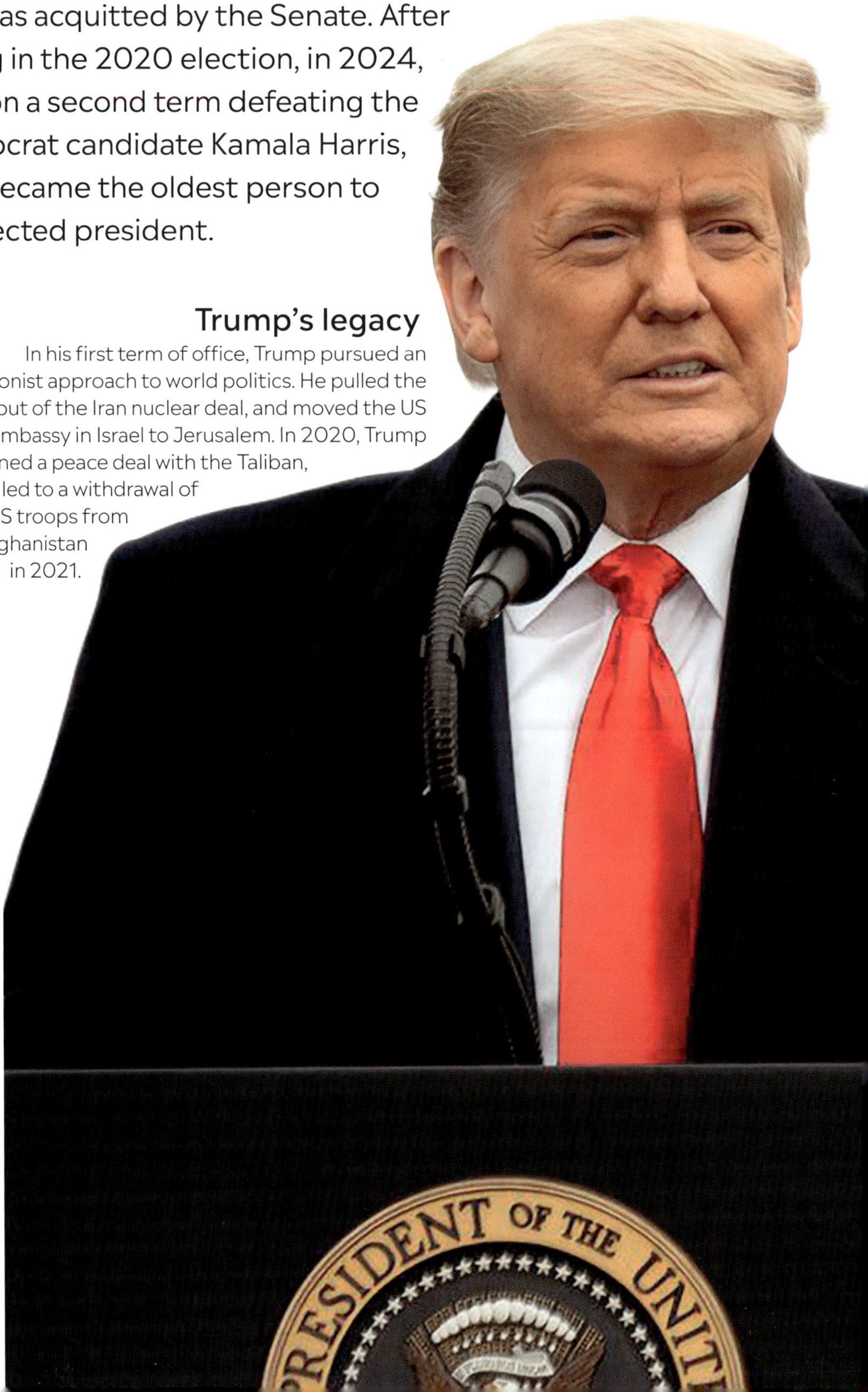

Trump's legacy
In his first term of office, Trump pursued an isolationist approach to world politics. He pulled the US out of the Iran nuclear deal, and moved the US Embassy in Israel to Jerusalem. In 2020, Trump signed a peace deal with the Taliban, which led to a withdrawal of all US troops from Afghanistan in 2021.

Protectionism
President Trump (seen here with Chinese leader Xi Jinping on a state visit to Beijing) pursued global trade deals aimed at protecting US industries from foreign competition. He advocated and implemented taxing imports, particularly from China.

Tough talk
"You gotta start paying your bills," said Trump to NATO allies, asking them to increase their defence spending to meet the minimum amount they had agreed on. In Trump's first term, only 5 countries hit the target, but by 2024, 23 countries met the guideline.

Immigration
Trump's administration pursued controversial tactics to reduce immigration. Early in his first term, Trump attempted to block immigrants from majority-Muslim countries in what is now known as "the Muslim ban". Another policy saw young children separated from their families at the southern border (above).

The Supreme Court
During his first term, Trump was able to appoint three justices to the Supreme Court, using these appointments to bring the conservative values of his campaign to the federal government. He nominated Neil Gorsuch and Brett Kavanaugh, and even got a third, Amy Coney Barrett (above), confirmed just before the 2020 presidential election.

Second victory
After surviving two assassination attempts during his campaign, Trump swept to victory in the 2024 election, becoming only the second president to serve two nonconsecutive terms. He won voters over with his message on the immigration crisis at the US-Mexico border and with his promises to address issues such as inflation.

Vice President Vance
Senator J D Vance was selected as Trump's running mate to help win over the working-class vote. He was known for his memoir *Hillbilly Elegy*, published in 2016, which focused on the poverty in Middletown, Ohio, where he grew up. He espouses strong conservative opinions opposing abortion, LGBTQ+ rights, and gun control.

Joe **Biden**

JOSEPH R BIDEN

46TH PRESIDENT
2021-2025

BORN
20 November 1942
Scranton, Pennsylvania

INAUGURATED AS PRESIDENT
20 January 2021

AGE AT INAUGURATION
78

PARTY
Democratic

FIRST LADY
Jill Biden

CHILDREN
Beau, Hunter
Naomi, Ashley

A former senator and vice president, Joe Biden offered calm, compassion, and experience to an America weary of controversies. Biden's nearly 50 years in government encouraged the belief that he could address the nation's many difficulties, from systemic racism to the coronavirus pandemic and climate change.

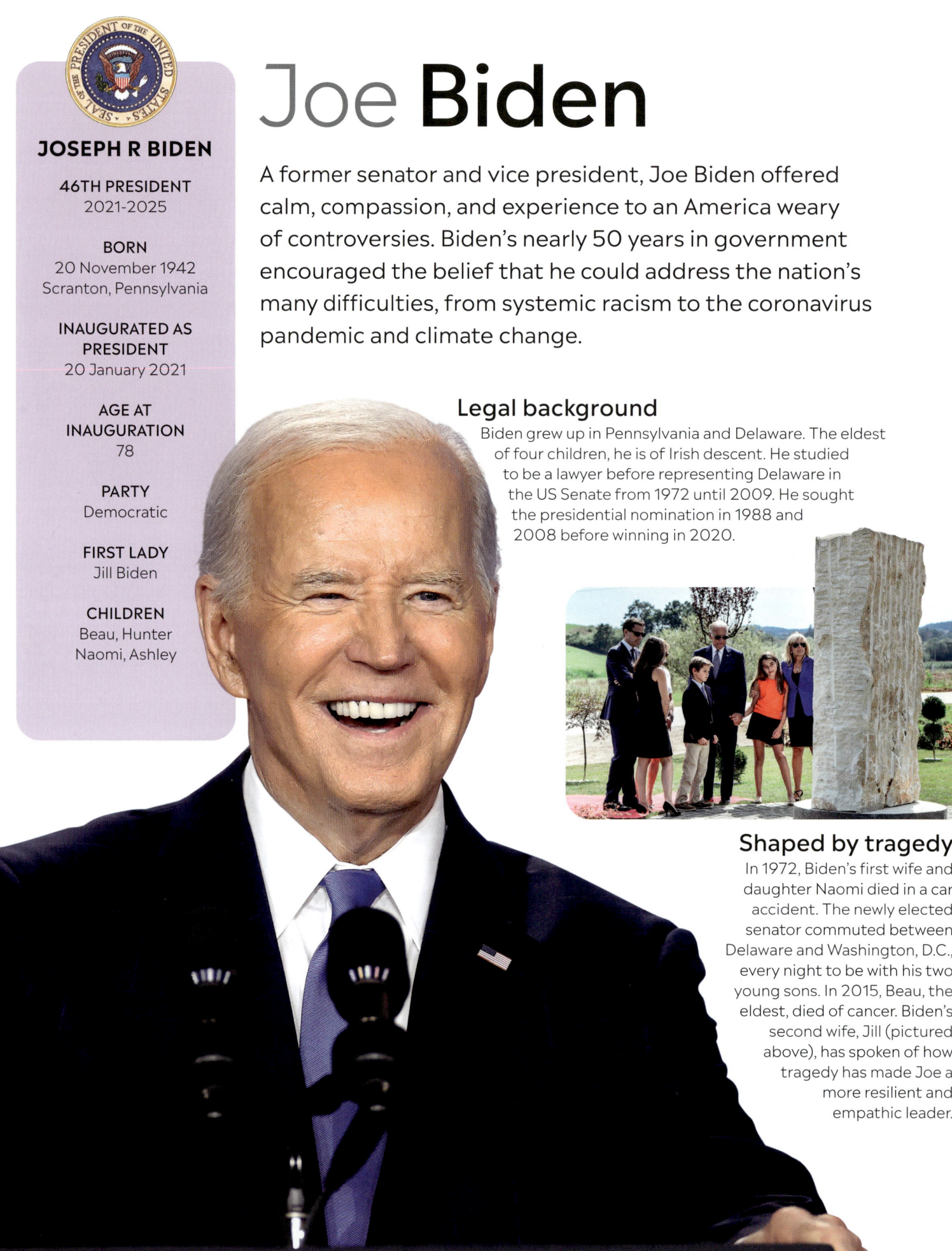

Legal background
Biden grew up in Pennsylvania and Delaware. The eldest of four children, he is of Irish descent. He studied to be a lawyer before representing Delaware in the US Senate from 1972 until 2009. He sought the presidential nomination in 1988 and 2008 before winning in 2020.

Shaped by tragedy
In 1972, Biden's first wife and daughter Naomi died in a car accident. The newly elected senator commuted between Delaware and Washington, D.C., every night to be with his two young sons. In 2015, Beau, the eldest, died of cancer. Biden's second wife, Jill (pictured above), has spoken of how tragedy has made Joe a more resilient and empathic leader.

A long career in politics

As vice president Biden supported the Iran nuclear deal and backed the Paris Agreement on climate change. At home, he oversaw the Recovery Act's clean energy investment and helped get the Affordable Care Act passed. As president, Biden voiced his support for the Black Lives Matter movement and LGBTQ+ rights.

Ketanji Brown Jackson

Biden nominated Ketanji Brown Jackson to replace the retiring Justice Stephen Breyer. Jackson is the first Black woman to serve as a Supreme Court Justice. Biden called her "one of the nation's brightest legal minds".

Inflation control

In August 2022, Biden signed the "Inflation Reduction Act", which cut prescription drug prices, created opportunities for investment in renewable energy sources, and provided money for infrastructure projects to promote sustainable transport.

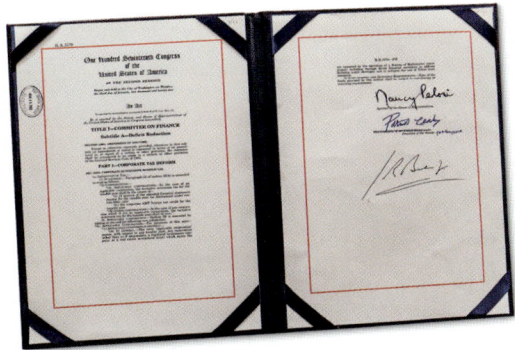

Biden observes a quantum computer at the IBM facility in Poughkeepsie, New York.

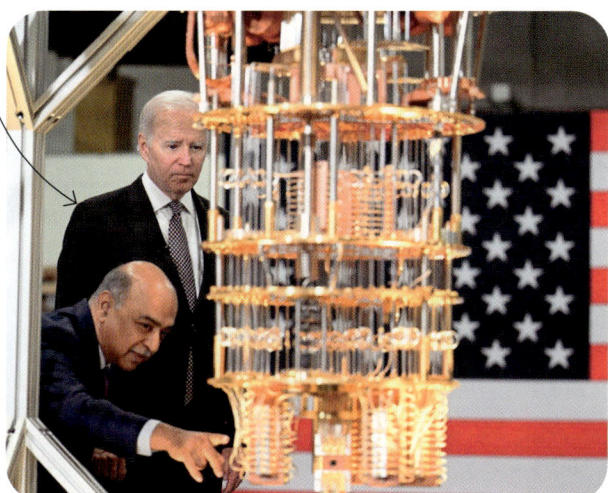

CHIPS and Science Act

Biden's CHIPS and Science Act led to increased production of semiconductors in the US, with new plants opening in Arizona. Companies have pledged $825 million in support.

Campaign for a second term

Biden ended his re-election campaign on 21 July 2024, after a debate performance that led to questions about his age and health. He endorsed Vice President Kamala Harris as the presidential nominee.

Jill Biden

First Lady Jill Biden supported military families through the Joining Forces programme, which she started with former First Lady Michelle Obama in 2011. In 2023, she launched a White House initiative to increase research and funding for women's health issues.

Presidential speeches

Presidents have always given speeches to calm the public's fears, inspire citizens to action, and account for their decisions. Some of these speeches have stood the test of time. The following excerpts from presidential speeches show how words can make a difference.

GEORGE WASHINGTON

George Washington's Farewell Address, published in newspapers on 19 September 1796, was an open letter to the public. He told citizens that he would not seek a third term. Above all, the much-loved first president cautioned Americans to work to preserve their hard-won independence.

...The unity of government which constitutes you one people is also now dear to you. It is justly so, for it is a main pillar in the edifice of your real independence, the support of your tranquility at home, your peace abroad; of your safety; of your prosperity; of that very liberty which you so highly prize. But as it is easy to foresee that, from different causes and from different quarters, much pains will be taken, many artifices employed to weaken in your minds the conviction of this truth; as this is the point in your political fortress against which the batteries of internal and external enemies will be most constantly and actively (though often covertly and insidiously) directed, it is of infinite moment that you should properly estimate the immense value of your national union to your collective and individual happiness...

An engraving depicting Washington's Farewell Address

ABRAHAM LINCOLN

Abraham Lincoln's Gettysburg Address, 19 November 1863

The world will little note nor long remember what we say here, but it can never forget what they did here. It is for us the living rather to be dedicated here to the unfinished work which they who fought here have thus far so nobly advanced. It

Lincoln at Gettysburg Cemetery

Printed copy of address

is rather for us to be here dedicated to the great task remaining before us – that from these honoured dead we take increased devotion to that cause for which they gave the last full measure of devotion – that we here highly resolve that these dead shall not have died in vain, that this nation, under God, shall have a new birth of freedom, and that the government of the people, by the people, and for the people, shall not perish from the earth.

FRANKLIN D ROOSEVELT

Franklin D Roosevelt's First Inaugural Address, 4 March 1933

...This is preeminently the time to speak the truth...frankly and boldly...This great Nation will endure as it has endured, will revive and will prosper. So, first of all, let me assert my firm belief that the only thing we have to fear is fear itself – nameless, unreasoning, unjustified terror which paralyzes needed efforts to convert retreat into advance. In every dark hour of our national life a leadership of frankness and vigour has met with that understanding and support of the people themselves which is essential to victory. I am convinced that you will again give that support to leadership in these critical days.

Roosevelt with Herbert Hoover on the way to his first inauguration

JOHN F KENNEDY

John F Kennedy's Inaugural Address, 20 January 1961

... [The] revolutionary beliefs for which our forebears fought are still at issue around the globe – the belief that the rights of man come not from the generosity of the state, but from the hand of God.

We dare not forget today that we are the heirs of that first revolution. Let the word go forth from this time and place, to friend and foe alike, that the torch has been passed to a new generation of Americans – born in this century, tempered by war, disciplined by a hard and bitter peace, proud of our ancient heritage – and unwilling to witness or permit the slow undoing of those human rights to which this Nation has always been committed, and to which we are committed today at home and around the world ...

In the long history of the world, only a few generations have been granted the role of defending freedom in its hour of maximum danger. I do not shrink from this responsibility – I welcome it. I do not believe that any of us would exchange places with any other people or any other generation. The energy, the faith, the devotion which we bring to this endeavor will light our country and all who serve it – and the glow from that fire can truly light the world.

And so, my fellow Americans: ask not what your country can do for you – ask what you can do for your country.

My fellow citizens of the world: ask not what America will do for you, but what together we can do for the freedom of man.

JFK with Peace Corps volunteers

RONALD REAGAN

Ronald Reagan's Evil Empire Speech, 8 March 1983

... I urge you to speak out against those who would place the United States in a position of military and moral inferiority ... I urge you to beware the temptation of pride – the temptation to blithely declare yourselves above it all and label both sides equally at fault, to ignore the facts of history and the aggressive impulses of an evil empire, to simply call the arms race a giant misunderstanding and ... remove yourself from the struggle between right and wrong and good and evil ...

... [T]he struggle now going on for the world will never be decided by bombs or rockets, by armies or military might. The real crisis we face today is a spiritual one; at root, it is a test of moral will and faith ...

I believe we shall rise to the challenge. I believe that communism is another sad, bizarre chapter in human history whose last pages even now are being written. I believe this because the source of our strength in the quest for human freedom is not material, but spiritual. And because it knows no limitation, it must terrify and ultimately triumph over those who would enslave their fellow man.

Reagan at the podium

PRESIDENTIAL FIRSTS

- Andrew Jackson was the first president to survive an assassination attempt.
- Martin Van Buren was the first president born in the United States.
- John Tyler was the first vice president to rise to the presidency upon the death of a president.
- Grover Cleveland was the first president to have a child born in the White House.
- William McKinley was the first president to ride in an automobile.
- Theodore Roosevelt was the first American to win the Nobel Peace Prize.
- Harry S Truman was the first president to give a speech on television.
- Lyndon B Johnson was the first president to name a Black person to his cabinet.
- Barack Obama was the first biracial president.

BOOKS BY PRESIDENTS

- Ulysses S Grant's *Personal Memoirs* relates his experiences in the Civil War.
- *The Rough Riders,* by Theodore Roosevelt, is based on his diary kept during the Spanish-American War.
- Dwight Eisenhower's *Crusade in Europe* recounts his experiences in World War II.
- John F Kennedy's *Profiles in Courage* highlights the work of great US senators.
- Jimmy Carter's *An Hour Before Daylight* tells the story of his childhood.
- George Bush's *Portraits of Courage: A Commander in Chief's Tribute to America's Warriors* features his paintings of wounded US veterans and their stories.
- Barack Obama's memoir *A Promised Land* gives an account of his time as president, including the search for Osama Bin Laden.

Index

ABC
Adams, Abigail 8
Adams, John 7, 8–9, 10, 11, 15
Adams, John Quincy 9, 15, 71
Affordable Care Act 64, 65, 69
Afghanistan 66
Alamo 17
Al-Qaeda 62, 63
American Revolution 4, 10
Arthur, Chester A. 31
assassinations 27, 31, 33, 49
 attempted 56, 67, 71
atomic bombs 42, 44, 45
banking 7, 37, 39, 40, 41
Berlin airlift 45
Berlin Wall 59
Biden, Jill 68, 69
Biden, Joe 68–69
Bill of Rights 14
bin Laden, Osama 62
Brown, John 23
Buchanan, James 22, 23
Bush, Barbara 58
Bush, George H. W. 58–59
Bush, George W. 62–63, 71
California 20, 21, 31, 35
Camp David Accords 55
Carter, Jimmy 54, 55, 71
Chesapeake, USS 13
China 31, 45, 52, 66
CHIPS and Science Act 69
Churchill, Winston 42, 43
civil rights 44, 47, 48, 49, 50, 67, 69
civil service 31
Civil War 24, 25, 26–27, 29, 30, 31, 71
Clark, William 13
Cleveland, Frances 32
Cleveland, Grover 32
Clinton, Hillary 60, 61, 64
Clinton, Bill 60–61
Cold War 45, 52, 56, 59
communism 45, 47, 59, 71
Confederate States 25, 26
Constitution 5, 14
 Thirteenth Amendment 28
 Sixteenth Amendment 36
 Nineteenth Amendment 37
Constitution, USS 9
Continental Congress 10, 11
Coolidge, Calvin 38, 39
Coolidge, Grace 38
Cuba 33, 34, 49

DEFG
Davis, Jefferson 25
Declaration of Independence 8, 10, 11
Democratic-Republicans 9
Douglass, Frederick 23
economy 31, 38, 55, 56, 58, 60, 67, 69
 depression 15, 18, 32, 39, 40
Eisenhower, Dwight D. 43, 46–47, 52, 71
Eisenhower, Mamie 46
environmentalism 35, 58, 59, 69
Fillmore, Millard 22
Ford, Betty 54
Ford, Gerald R. 54
Franklin, Benjamin 10, 11
Free-Soil Party 22, 23
Garfield, James A. 31
Gettysburg Address 27, 70
Gettysburg, battle of 25, 26
gold 21, 30
Gore, Al 60, 62
Grant, Ulysses S. 26, 27, 29, 71
Great Britain 4, 7, 8, 11, 13, 14, 20, 40
Great Depression 39, 40
Guadalupe Hidalgo, Treaty of 20
Gulf War 58, 59

HIJKL
Haiti 60
Hamilton, Alexander 7, 9, 13
Harding, Warren G. 38, 39
Harris, Kamala 66, 69
Harrison, Benjamin 32, 33
Harrison, William Henry 19, 33
Haudenosaunee Confederacy 7
Hawaii 33, 42
Hayes, Lucy 30
Hayes, Rutherford B. 30
Hermitage 16, 17
Hiroshima 44
Hoover, Herbert 39, 41, 70
Hussein, Saddam 59, 62, 63
immigration 31, 33, 67
impeachment 28, 53, 61, 66
Indigenous Peoples 7, 13, 18
Indian Removal Act 17
 battles 7, 17, 19, 21, 30
 Trail of Tears 17, 18
Iran 55, 57, 66, 69
Iraq 58, 59, 62, 63
Iwo Jima 43
Jackson, Andrew 16–17, 18, 71
Jefferson, Thomas 7, 9, 10–13
Johnson, Andrew 28
Johnson, Lyndon B. 50–51, 71
Kansas-Nebraska Act 22
Kennedy, Jackie 48, 49, 50
Kennedy, John F. 48–49, 50, 52, 60, 71
King, Jr., Martin Luther 49
Korean War 45, 46
Kosovo 61
Lakota 30
Lee, Gen. Robert E. 26, 27
Lewinsky, Monica 61
Lewis, Meriwether 13
Lincoln, Abraham 23, 24–27, 70
Lincoln, Mary Todd 24
Lindbergh, Charles 38
Little Rock 47
Louisiana Purchase 10, 13

MNOPQ
McCarthy, Joseph 47
McKinley, William 32, 33, 71
Madison, Dolley 14
Madison, James 14, 15
Mao Zedong 52
Marshall Plan 45
Mexican-American War 20, 21, 25
Mexico 17, 20, 37, 67
Monroe, James 15
Monticello 12
Mount Vernon 6
NATO 61, 67
New Deal 40, 41
New Orleans, battle of 14, 16
Nixon, Richard M. 46, 52–53, 54
nuclear weapons 49, 56, 66, 69
Obama, Barack 64–65, 71
Obama, Michelle 65, 69
Oppenheimer, J. Robert 42
Oregon 20
Panama 58
Paris, Treaty of 33
Pierce, Franklin 22, 25
Polk, James K. 20
Proclamation of Neutrality 7
Prohibition 37, 40

RS
Reagan, Nancy 57
Reagan, Ronald 56–57, 58, 71
Republican Party 23, 28, 31
Roosevelt, Eleanor 40
Roosevelt, Franklin D. 40–43, 44, 70
Roosevelt, Theodore 33, 34–35, 36, 71
Ross, John 17
Sacagawea 12, 13
Sagoyewatha 7
Scott, Dred 23
September 11 62, 63
slavery 6, 12, 13, 15, 16, 17, 19, 21, 22, 23, 24, 25
 abolitionists 22, 23, 25
 emancipation 25, 26, 28
Soviet Union 45, 46, 47, 48, 49, 52, 56
space race 47, 48, 52, 53
Spanish-American War 34
Stalin, Joseph 42, 43, 45
stock market crash 39
Stowe, Harriet Beecher 22
Supreme Court 5, 13, 23, 36, 47, 62, 67, 69

TUVW
Taft, William H. 36
Tasunke Witco 30
Tatanka Iyotanka, Chief 30
Taylor, Zachary 20, 21
Teapot Dome scandal 38
Texas 17, 20, 49
Tilden, Samuel J. 30
Truman, Harry S. 44–45, 71
Trump, Donald 61, 66–67
Tyler, John 19, 71
US Navy 8, 26, 33
Van Buren, Martin 18, 19, 58, 71
Vance, J. D. 67
Versailles, Treaty of 37
Vietnam War 50, 51, 52, 53, 54
Virginia, University of 12
Washington, Booker T. 35
Washington, D.C. 7, 9, 14
Washington, George 4–7, 70
Washington, Martha 6
Watergate 53
Whiskey Rebellion 6
White House 9, 14, 16, 35, 36, 46, 48
Wilson, Edith 37
Wilson, Woodrow 37
World War I 37
World War II 40, 42–44, 47, 48, 71

Acknowledgments

The publisher would like to thank the following people for their help with making the book:
Alan Reason for additional illustrations; Tina Chambers, Lynton Gardiner, Dave King, and Matthew Ward for additional photography; Hazel Beynon for editorial assistance; Vagisha Pushp for picture research assistance; Carron Brown for proofreading, indexing, and anglicization.

The publisher would like to thank the following for their kind permission to reproduce their photographs:
(key: t: top, b: bottom, l: left, r: right, c: centre, a: above)

Alamy Stock Photo: American Photo Archive 42c, Associated Press / Uncredited 49crb, BLM Collection 21cla, CBP Photos 67cla, Chicago History Museum 22tr, Chronicle 31br, Dpa Picture Alliance 69br, Evan El-Amin 61cr, Theo. Fuchs 30-31bc, GL Archive 45cl, GRANGER - Historical Picture Archive 38tr, 70bl, Hirarchivum Press 5br, incamerastock / ICP 26clb, ITAR-TASS News Agency 66clb, MPVHistory 5cla, Newscom / BJ Warnick 8-9bc, Painting 4bc, Reuters / Sylvia Buchholz 65tl (QUERY DOUBLE INSTANCE), Science History Images 11, Science History Images / Photo Researchers 57l, Ian Shaw 22ftl, Sipa US / MCT 63cl, UPI 67tr, Virginia Museum of History & Culture 40bc, Bill Waterson 49bl, World History Archive 40tr, World Politics Archive (WPA) 66-67, 69ca, Xinhua / Ting Shen 69tr; **Bettmann/Corbis:** 71tr, 71bc; **Bridgeman Art Library:** 6tr, 24b, 27c; **Bridgeman Images:** Ted Spiegel / GEO Image Collection 48b; **Camera Press:** 50tr; **/Wilberforce House, Hull City Museum:** 22tl; **Dreamstime.com:** Americanspirit 65clb, Arak7 37cll, Onur Ersin 5tr, Izanbar 14tl, Lightscribe 70crb, Timothy Nichols 27tc; **ET Archive:** 5b, 21cl; **Mary Evans Picture Library:** 6bl, 9tr, 12cla, bl, 17tl, 31br, 33br, 48tr; **Getty Images:** AFP / Thierry Charlier 67tl, AFP / Luke Frazza / Staff 61bl, AFP / Mandel Ngan 69cr, AFP / Mike Nelson 61tl, Archive Photos / Arnold Sachs 60br, Bettmann 49tl, Bettmann / Contributor 54cl, Brooks Kraft LLC / Sygma 62crb, Kevin Dietsch 68bl, M. Tran / FilmMagic 66bl, Anna Moneymaker 67cb, Armend Nimani / Stringer / Afp 68cr, Jeff Overs / Contributor / BBC News & Current Affairs 65cl, Paul J. Richards / AFP 65cr, Michael M. Santiago 69cl, Pete Souza / The White House 65br, Pictures From History / Universal Images Group 54br, Popperfoto 50-51b, Richard Cummins 66cl, The Chronicle Collection / Diana Walker 58-59b; **Andrew Gombert/epa/Corbis:** 64-5b; **Hulton Getty Images:** 44bl, c; **iStockphoto.com:** hept27 61tr; **Abbie Rowe, National Park Service:** 71c; **Library of Congress, Washington, D.C.:** 70tr, c, br LC-DIG-pga-07513 17cr; **Metropolitan Museum of Art, New York, U.S.A./ Bridgeman Art Library:** 4b; **NASA:** 53t; **Peter Newark's Pictures:** 6br, 7tl, tc, 10bl, 12-13, 14bl, 15tr, 18b, 22tr, cla, br, 23tr, bl, 32cr, 33tl, 35cl, 35br, 37bl, 38bl, bc, br, 40c, 42-3b, 45br, cr, 49crb, 50tl, 51cl, 53cl, 56tl; **Obama For America/Handout/Reuters/Corbis:** 64tr; **Penguin Random House:** ISBN 9780739370636 64bl; **Popperfoto:** 8-9b, 49tl, b, 50-lb, 60br; **Reuters/Corbis:** 63tl, cl, cr; **Courtesy of Smithsonian. ©2020 Smithsonian.:** 4tr, 7bl, 8bl, bl, 9br, 10br, tr, 13tr, 14br, 15bra, 16cl, 17tr, 18tr, trb, 19tl, br, 23c, 24tr, c, Division of Social History, Political History / National Museum of American History / Behring Center 24fcl, National Museum of American History 24cl, 27cb, cr, br, 28tl, ca, cb, 30tl, 31ca, 32t, 33bca, 35tr, bl, 36bca, 37br, 39tc, crb, 40bc, 41tc, 43tc, tr, br, 46cl, cra, crb, b, er, 49tr, 52tl, cla, clb, 53c, 54tl, 55tc, ca, cb, 56cl, 58ca, cb, 60bc, crb, 61trb, c, cb, 62ca, bl, **/National Museum of American History:** 2cra, 5crb, 7cr, 9tl, 10tl, 12clb, 16tc, tr, 17bl, 19bc, 22bl, 28br, 30cl, 32br, 34cla, tlb, tr, 35c, 37tcr, cra, ca, 50bc, br, 53cb; **/National Portrait Gallery:** 5tl, 6c, 7cl, bl, 8t, 10tr, 14tr, 15tl, c, bl, br, 18tl, 19c, bl, 20tr, 20-21b, 21tr, 22cr, 23cl, cr, 25bl, 26cl, bl, 26-7b, 27tr, 28tr, cl, b, 29tl, tr, br, bl, 30tr, bl, 31cb, 32bl, 33tr, cl, 34b, 36tl, c, 37cr, 38tl, cl, 39cl, 40ll, 44bl, 45tr, 47bl, 52b, c, 54cr, 55br, 56bl, 58tl; **/ Rex by Shutterstock:** Greg Gibson / AP 64c, Patrick Semansky / AP 69tl; **Shutterstock.com:** Phil Mistry 67br; **Rosalind Solomon:** 57br; **/Diana Walter:** 58-59lb; **Science & Society Picture Library:** 30cr; **Steven Starr/Corbis:** 65tc; **Topham Picturepoint:** 1, 14cl, 25t, 39b, 40-lb, 41cr, 42tl, 43cr, 44cr, 47tl, tr, 51t, 53b, 55cl, bl, 56cr, br, 57tr, c, 58tr, 59c, 60c, 61tr; **University of Pittsburgh / ULS Digital Collections:** Paul Slantis Photographs 46tr; **The US National Archives and Records Administration:** Office for Emergency Management, War Production Board 43tr; **Valdrin Xhemaj/epa/Corbis:** 63b; **White House Historical Association:** George W. Bush Presidential Library and Museum 62tl

Wallchart: Alamy Stock Photo: GL Archive (Carter, Reagan), Auk Archive (Jackson), CPA Media Pte Ltd / Pictures From History (Benjamin), DappledHistory.com (Buren, Cleveland, Taft), dbtravel (Buchanan, Grant), GRANGER - Historical Picture Archive. (Coolidge, Ford), Heritage Image Partnership Ltd (Garfield), Hi-Story (Arthur, Johnson, Eisenhower), IanDagnall Computing (Adams, Jefferson, Harrison, Tyler, Taylor, Fillmore, Harding, Bush, Obama, Biden), incamerastock / ICP (Polk), MPVHistory (Washington), Niday Picture Library (Madison), (Quincy), North Wind Picture Archives (Wilson), Painting (Monroe), Pictorial Press Ltd (Roosevelt, Franklin, Truman, Lyndon, Clinton), Science History Images / Photo Researchers (Hoover), SIPA USA (George W), Stocktrek Images, Inc. (Hayes, McKinley), Bill Waterson (Nixon), World History Archive (Kennedy); **Bridgeman Images:** Huntington Art Collections / © Huntington Library, Art Museum, and Botanical Gardens (Lincoln); **Library of Congress, Washington, D.C.:** LC-DIG-ppbd-0060 / Craighead, Shealah, photographer (Trump); **Shutterstock.com:** Everett Collection (Pierce)

Cover images: *Front:* **Alamy Stock Photo:** Alto Vintage Images fclb, CPA Media Pte Ltd ftl, Michael Flippo - Sports Images cla, GRANGER - Historical Picture Archive tr, br, Alan Wilson c, YA / BOT cb; **Getty Images:** Bettmann fcla, Heritage Art / Heritage Images ftr, Jeff Overs cra, SSPL tl; **National Museum of American History / Smithsonian Institution:** Maxine Perkins and Maggie Rothschild fcr, cr; *Back:* **Alamy Stock Photo:** Chronicle tl; **Division of Work and Industry, National Museum of American History, Smithsonian Institution:** tr; **Getty Images:** Photo12 / Universal Images Group cr, Smith Collection / Gado cl; *Spine:* **Alamy Stock Photo:** Alan Wilson

 # WHAT WILL YOU EYEWITNESS NEXT?

 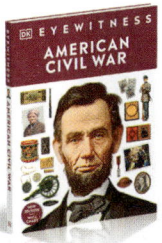 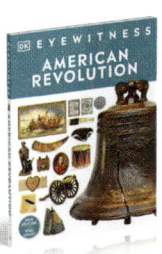 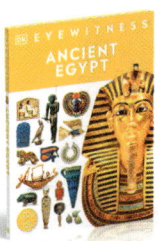   

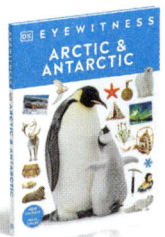    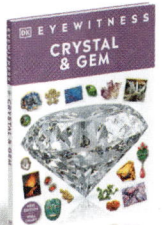  

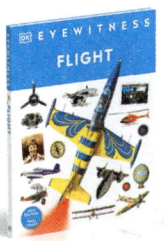    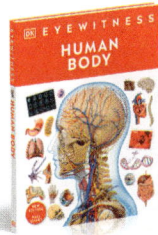 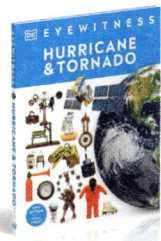 

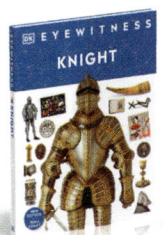   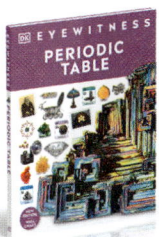   

    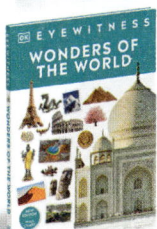 

Also available:

Eyewitness Bible Lands   Eyewitness Shakespeare   Eyewitness Victorians
Eyewitness Forensic Science   Eyewitness Tudor